MOONLIGHTING

A COOKBOOK AND CULINARY HISTORY

Recipes, Restaurants, Clubs, and Cocktails
Featured in the Iconic 1980s Series

MOONLIGHTING

A COOKBOOK AND CULINARY HISTORY

Recipes, Restaurants, Clubs, and Cocktails
Featured in the Iconic 1980s Series

CAROLYN MERRITT GANDY

TUCKER
DS
PRESS

Moonlighting A Cookbook And Culinary History © 2025 Carolyn Merritt Gandy

All Rights Reserved.

Reproduction in whole or in part without the author's permission is strictly forbidden. This book is a scholarly look at *Moonlighting* and has no affiliation with ABC, ABC Circle Films, or Picturemaker Productions. All photos and/or copyrighted material appearing in this book remain the work of its owners.

Cover design by Claire Gandy
Edited by David Bushman
Book designed by Scott Ryan
Moonlighting photos courtesy of ABC
Matchbooks and menus courtesy of Los Angeles Public Library's Digital Menus Collection

Published in the USA by Tucker DS Press
Columbus, Ohio

Contact Information
Email: TuckerDSPress@gmail.com
Website: TuckerDSPress.com
Instagram: @Fayettevillemafiapress

To Darren:
You are the butter to my bread
and the breath to my life.
I love you.

CONTENTS

Introduction..1

Chapter 1   Cocktails..4

Chapter 2   Appetizers & First Courses............................35

Chapter 3   Main Courses...54

Chapter 4   Desserts...82

Chapter 5   Breakfast...95

Chapter 6   *Moonlighting* Restaurants & Nightclubs: A History.......103

Chapter 7   The Straight Poop..137

Acknowledgments...148

About the Author...150

-INTRODUCTION-

I vividly remember the first time I watched *Moonlighting*, the iconic series created by Glenn Gordon Caron, starring Cybill Shepherd and Bruce Willis, that aired on ABC from 1985 to 1989. It was March 1985, and I had just turned sixteen years old. My father—a Cybill Shepherd fan from her movies *Taxi Driver* and *The Last Picture Show* and an earlier series she had starred in called *The Yellow Rose*—had suggested we watch the pilot. The moment Maddie Hayes walked into David Addison's office and that pail fell on Agnes' head—and David said, "We're looking a bit pail today, aren't we, Miss Dipesto?"—I knew this show was unlike anything I'd ever seen before on television. The chemistry between Maddie and David was electric and palpable, the dialogue was fast-paced and intelligent, and the format was a mix of comedy and drama, one of television's earlier "dramedies." I was instantly hooked and have been for almost forty years.

Moonlighting was one of the hottest shows on television in the 1980s and, moreover, a cultural phenomenon. At 9:00 p.m. EST every Tuesday night, you could hear a pin drop as people gathered around their televisions to watch the latest "will they, won't they" episode with Maddie and David. These were of course the days before streaming, so you had to watch it live—or record it on your VCR. I still have every episode of the show recorded on VHS tapes!

The impact of *Moonlighting* was huge, from fashion to music to dialogue. It was, quite simply, one of the hippest and hottest shows on television, and that was reflected by both its ratings and its impact on popular culture. The Motown music featured in *Moonlighting* episodes had a resurgence. David Addison wore Ray-Ban Wayfarer sunglasses and suddenly so did everyone else. Those soft pastel suits and belted dresses that Maddie Hayes wore were a part of trendsetting American fashion. Guys wanted to *be* David Addison, and girls wanted to be *with* David Addison. The show's dialogue, smart and funny, has permeated American vernacular to this day: "No flies on you." "Do bears bear? Do bees be?" "I don't give a flying fig" are all bits of *Moonlighting* dialogue that I use in everyday life almost forty years later.

Bruce Willis was a virtual unknown when he was cast to play David Addison—he had been a stage actor and bartender in New York City before moving to Los Angeles and had, prior to *Moonlighting*, guest starred in an episode of *Miami Vice*, another popular 1980s series. Cybill Shepherd had had an illustrious career as a model and film star before taking the television role that would reignite her career. The chemistry between Cybill and Bruce as Maddie and David is the stuff of legend—it is absolutely electric on-screen.

Much has been written about the infamous "*Moonlighting* Curse"— whereby a show jumps the shark after its protagonists sleep together— but I don't buy the logic. This "curse" has plagued this series for years and influenced how television romances played out in other series for years to come.

After the magic of the first three seasons, *Moonlighting* fell victim to what can only be characterized as bad timing and a series of unfortunate events. Unusually long filming days and a pattern of writing and rewriting shows right up until the moment that scenes were filmed added spontaneity to the show but led to burnout by everyone involved. Internal arguments about the best plans for the characters and plots added to the stress of producing the show. A writers' strike, Cybill's pregnancy with twins, and a little movie called *Die Hard* just added to the complexities that *Moonlighting* faced. Moreover, the network television series model of the day, which expected twenty-two episodes per season, with a broadcast calendar running from September to May, wasn't a good fit with *Moonlighting*'s frantic, up-to–the-last-minute production pace—the series would have benefited from today's streaming production schedules of fewer episodes per season and longer breaks between seasons. But at its best, *Moonlighting* was some of the finest television ever produced. It was lightning in a bottle and, quite simply, magic.

As I've rewatched *Moonlighting* over the years, I've realized just how integral food and drinks are to this show—more than in any other series I've ever seen. Meals with clients . . . Blue Moon office events . . . nights out on the town with family and friends . . . David's drunken escapades and lost weekends: so many of *Moonlighting*'s most memorable moments center on food and drinks. The series also is in many ways a time capsule of the food-and-drink culture of America and, in particular, Los Angeles, in the 1980s.

I hope this cookbook reminds you of your favorite memories and scenes from *Moonlighting* and makes you nostalgic for 1980s cocktails and cuisine.

David: "Thought I heard you kids out there. Hi Sweet Cakes! This your business dinner? Hi, I'm Papa Bear. Come on in and have some Tang. We just made some fresh." From "Read the Mind, See the Movie," Season 1, Episode 3

– CHAPTER 1 –
Cocktails

David: "I need a drink. Does anybody else need a drink?"
Maddie: "I know I do." From "Every Daughter's Father Is a Virgin," Season 2, Episode 14

There isn't a single episode of *Moonlighting* without some reference to cocktails or drinking. Whether at client meetings or dinners with family, during nights out with colleagues or David's crazy bar escapades and lost weekends, drinks permeate the culture and mood of the series. Some of the most iconic scenes circle around nights out on the town: David singing Aretha Franklin's "Respect" after one too many tequilas in "The Next Murder You Hear"; Maddie, David, and Richie out dancing and having drinks in "Brother, Can You Spare a Blonde?"; Maddie and Agnes going out for cocktails "like the boy detectives do" in "I Am Curious, Maddie." The list goes on and on!

The following cocktail recipes are all inspired by characters or scenes from the show. All of the recipes featured make one cocktail unless otherwise specified.

The David

The David is inspired by a classic old-fashioned cocktail: strong, seductive, hip, cool, and slightly mysterious, but also dependable—just like David Addison himself.

    2 teaspoons simple syrup (see recipe below)
    2 ounces high quality, small batch bourbon
    3 dashes Angostura bitters
    3 dashes orange bitters
    1 piece orange peel

In a lowball glass, add the simple syrup, bourbon, Angostura bitters, and orange bitters. Stir for one minute until the ingredients are well combined. Add ice cubes (a single, large, perfect ice cube would be great here).

Spritz an orange peel over the glass. To do this, light a match and hold the colored side of the orange peel towards the flame to release its natural oils. Put out the flame, twist the peel, and add the peel to the drink.

To make the simple syrup: add one part sugar and one part water to a small saucepan and heat over medium heat, stirring frequently, until the sugar is dissolved. Cool and pour into a jar or a squeeze bottle. You can store the leftovers in the fridge for up to one month.

The Maddie

The Maddie is inspired by a white lady cocktail but made with vodka instead of gin. A white lady is a classic (and classy) drink invented in the 1920s at Harry's New York Bar in Paris. This version is an homage to the always classy, beautiful, and strong Maddie Hayes.

> 2 ounces high quality vodka, chilled
> 1/2 ounce Cointreau
> 1/2 ounce freshly squeezed lemon juice
> 1/4 ounce simple syrup
> 1 egg white
> 1 thin slice lemon peel

Add the vodka, Cointreau, lemon juice, simple syrup, and egg white to a shaker and dry shake (without ice) vigorously. Add ice and shake again until well chilled.

Strain into a chilled coupe cocktail glass. Garnish with the lemon peel.

The Agnes

The Agnes is a tropical cocktail inspired by a classic mai tai. It packs a punch—we know Agnes loves a strong drink! It's a little fruity and a little nutty, just like our beloved Miss Dipesto.

> 3 ounces pineapple juice
> 2 ounces orange juice
> 1 1/2 ounces spiced rum
> 1/2 ounce coconut rum
> 1/2 ounce orgeat syrup
> 1 teaspoon grenadine syrup
> Orange slice, maraschino cherry, pineapple slice for garnish
> Accoutrements: Drink umbrella, straw, cocktail pick

In a cocktail shaker filled with ice, add the pineapple juice, orange juice, spiced rum, coconut rum, orgeat, and grenadine. Shake well for thirty seconds.

Strain the mixture into a hurricane glass filled with crushed ice. Garnish with a fruit pick with an orange slice, pineapple slice, and maraschino cherry; a drink umbrella; and a straw.

The Bert

The Bert is a cognac-based cocktail inspired by a classic sidecar, one of the cocktails favored by the Rat Pack and old Hollywood. Bert himself is a complex character—intelligent, funny, loyal, hardworking, sometimes cocky and at other times insecure and vulnerable. He idolizes Mr. Addison and tries to be as cool and hip as he is. Bert is David's sidekick—the sidecar to David's motorcycle.

1 1/2 ounces cognac
3/4 ounce Cointreau
3/4 ounce freshly squeezed lemon juice
Garnish: orange peel twist and sugar (for glass rim)

Coat the rim of a coupe glass with sugar and set aside.
    Fill a shaker with ice and add the cognac, Cointreau, and lemon juice and shake until well chilled, about thirty seconds.
    Strain into the prepared glass and garnish with an orange peel.

The Blue Moon

Inspired by the *Moonlighting* Pilot, Season 1, Episode 1

The Blue Moon is a classic cocktail invented during Hollywood's Golden Age. It is a perfect cocktail to play tribute to Blue Moon Detective Agency and to the Blue Moon Shampoo Girl herself, Maddie Hayes. This cocktail is simple yet very special, like drinking a "tablespoon of moonbeams."

> 2/3 ounce freshly squeezed lemon juice
> 2/3 ounce crème de violette
> 2 ounces high quality dry gin

Combine all the ingredients into a cocktail shaker. Add ice and shake well for thirty seconds. Strain into a small chilled coupe-style cocktail glass. Garnish with a lemon peel.

Kamikaze

David: "Here, drink this."
Maddie: "What is it?"
David: "A little kamikaze to take the edge off." From the "Pilot," Season 1, Episode 1

ABC Network Executive: "It's kamikaze time." From "Cool Hand Dave, Part 2," Season 4, Episode 6

The kamikaze was invented during World War II in a pub in an occupied American naval garrison in Japan. "Kamikaze" is a Japanese word that means "divine wind."

The drink became very popular in the 1970s. It was initially served as a shot, until bartenders converted it into a martini-style cocktail. It is just the sort of popular 1970s drink that David Addison would have served during his bartender days in New York City.

1 1/2 ounces vodka
1 ounce triple sec
1 ounce freshly squeezed lime juice
Lime wedge, for garnish

Fill a cocktail shaker with ice cubes and pour in the vodka, triple sec, and lime juice. Shake well and strain into a chilled martini-style glass. Garnish with a lime wedge.

Long Island Iced Tea

In the *Moonlighting* pilot, David and Maddie meet with Mrs. Kaplan following the death of her husband to try to get more information about the mysterious watch. Mrs. Kaplan is sitting by her pool and enjoying a Long Island iced tea, an extremely popular drink in the 1980s. This is a deceptively strong drink that sneaks up on you!

- 1/2 ounce vodka
- 1/2 ounce light rum
- 1/2 ounce gin
- 1/2 ounce tequila
- 1/2 ounce triple sec or Cointreau
- 1 ounce sweet and sour mix
- 1 ounce cola, or to taste
- 1 lemon slice

Add the vodka, rum, gin, tequila, triple sec, sweet and sour mix, and cola to a shaker filled with ice. Shake until well blended and cold, about thirty seconds. Serve in a highball glass over crushed ice, with a straw. Garnish with a lemon slice.

Vodka Gimlet

In season one's "Next Stop Murder," David and Maddie find themselves stuck on J. B. Harland's Murder Train along with Miss Dipesto. They try to make the most of it. At cocktail hour, the guests are served vodka gimlets and glasses of brandy.

A gimlet is a classic gin cocktail that became popular in the 1950s after it was featured in the 1953 Raymond Chandler novel *The Long Goodbye*. The vodka gimlet became extremely popular in the 1980s, along with many other vodka-based drinks.

2 ounces vodka
3/4 ounce freshly squeezed lime juice
1/2 ounce simple syrup
Lime peel, to garnish

Add the vodka, lime juice, and simple syrup to a cocktail shaker filled with ice. Shake until well chilled, about 30 seconds. Strain into a chilled coupe cocktail glass. Garnish with the lime peel.

Bunsen Burner

Rodney, to Miss Dipesto: "It's called a Bunsen Burner. Very lively. Very lethal. Here's to a beautiful woman, a good murder, and the man who brought us all together, J. B. Harland." From "Next Stop Murder," Season 1, Episode 5

In season one's "Next Stop Murder," J. B. Harland's assistant, Rodney, prepares this cocktail for Agnes. The Bunsen burner cocktail is a *Moonlighting* invention—I cannot find any other references to it in popular culture.

    2 ounces vodka
    3/4 ounce blue curaçao
    2 ounces pineapple juice
    1/2 ounce lime juice
    1/2 ounce lemon juice
    1/2 ounce simple syrup

Add all ingredients to a cocktail shaker filled with ice. Shake until well mixed. Strain into an old-fashioned glass—or, for a touch of whimsy, a beaker, like Rodney and Agnes do—filled with ice cubes.

Bloody Mary

David: "Give me a Bloody Mary. Easy on the blood. Heavy on the Mary."
From "Atlas Shrugged," Season 2, Episode 9

A Bloody Mary is a classic brunch cocktail made with tomato juice, vodka, and spices and is a favorite of David Addison's. David orders one after learning about Maddie's plans to sell the agency in season two's "Atlas Belched." He orders one again when Maddie's father takes him out to lunch to confront him about the baby and what he's going to do next in season four's "Father Knows Last." Can you blame David? I might have needed something stronger!

2 ounces vodka
4 ounces tomato juice
2 teaspoons prepared horseradish
2 dashes Worcestershire sauce
2 dashes Tabasco sauce, or any hot sauce you like

1 pinch ground black pepper
1 pinch smoked paprika
1 pinch celery salt
1 lime wedge
1 lemon wedge

Optional garnishes: celery stick and pimiento stuffed olives

Fill a cocktail shaker with ice. Squeeze in the lemon and lime wedges. Add the vodka, tomato juice, horseradish, Worcestershire, hot sauce, and spices. Shake well. Pour into a tall glass filled with ice cubes. Garnish with a celery stick or olives and serve.

Banana Daiquiri

David: "No date on a Friday night? The day people get paid, the night people get what rhymes with paid, the first night of the rest of your weekend."
Maddie: "I had a date. He had to go to a wedding. His own. He said he met her yesterday. Something about sharing an umbrella in the rain. Two straws in a banana daiquiri. Living a lifetime in one night."
From "The Bride of Tupperman," Season 2, Episode 11

In "The Bride of Tupperman," Maddie's date cancels after an impromptu wedding—his own! It's Friday night, and Maddie and David consider going out together before a client derails those plans.

A daiquiri is a classic tropical drink made with lime juice. Variations include strawberry, mango, and, here, banana.

Half of a large banana, sliced
1 ounce light rum
1 ounce freshly squeezed lime juice
1/2 ounce triple sec or Cointreau
1/2 cup coconut milk
1 teaspoon sugar, or to taste
1 cup crushed ice

Add all the ingredients to a blender and blend until smooth, about one minute. Pour into a daiquiri or other tall glass and serve.

Strawberry Margarita

David and Maddie each go their own way to find the perfect match for Mr. Tupperman in "The Bride of Tupperman." David visits the Beverly Hills restaurant En Brochette (now Il Cielo) to try to convince a beautiful woman to accept Mr. Tupperman's proposal and finds himself on the receiving end of a strawberry margarita dumped on his head by one of the patrons!

> 2 ounces tequila
> 1 ounce freshly squeezed lime juice
> 1 ounce triple sec or Cointreau
> 6 fresh, ripe strawberries, washed and hulled

For an on-the-rocks drink, muddle the strawberries in the bottom of a cocktail shaker. Add the remaining ingredients and add ice cubes. Shake until well chilled, about thirty seconds. Fine strain the mixture into a rocks glass or margarita glass filled with ice. Garnish with a fresh strawberry.

For a frozen drink, add the ingredients to a blender along with one cup of crushed ice. Blend well and pour into a margarita glass. Garnish with a fresh strawberry.

The Flying Fig

Maddie: "I don't give a flying fig about the lines in my face, the crows' feet by my eyes, or the altitude of my caboose."
David: "Hey, that's okay. That's what you got me for."
Maddie: "And I don't give a flying fig about people who do."
David: "Well I'm at a loss. I don't know what a flying fig is."
Maddie: "That's okay—they do."
(Maddie and David look at the camera, breaking the fourth wall. David winks.)
From "In God We Strongly Suspect" Season 2, Episode 13

2 ounces bourbon
1 ounce Cointreau
2 dried figs, quartered
1 teaspoon honey
4 ounces sparkling nonalcoholic apple cider
Pinch of Maldon Salt
1 sprig thyme, for garnish

Add the bourbon, Cointreau, figs, honey, and Maldon salt to a cocktail shaker filled with ice. Shake well for one minute.

Strain into a highball glass filled with ice cubes. Top with the sparkling cider and garnish with a sprig of thyme.

Tequila Sunrise

Inspired by "The Son Also Rises," Season 3, Episode 1

A tequila sunrise was an incredibly popular brunch cocktail in the 1980s. It's just the sort of drink that David would have enjoyed on his vacation in Mexico!

2 ounces tequila
4 ounces good quality orange juice (preferably fresh squeezed)
1/4 ounce grenadine
Orange slice and maraschino cherry for garnish

Fill a highball glass with ice. Add the tequila and then the orange juice. Top with the grenadine, which will sink to the bottom of the glass, creating a layered effect. Do not stir! Garnish with an orange slice and a cherry.

Boilermaker

David: "I just thought something a little more fun might be in order, like boilermakers, pretzels, dancing transvestites..."
From "Symphony in Knocked Flat" Season 2 Episode 3

A boilermaker is about as straightforward and easy a drink as you can get. Its roots go back to the 1800s factory workers who manufactured the boilers for locomotive engines and involves nothing more than a shot of whiskey dropped into a beer.

> 1 shot whiskey, bourbon, or Scotch
> 1 pint glass, filled with the beer of your choice
> (a nice lager, pale ale, or IPA works well here)

Typically, you will fill a pint glass halfway with beer, drop a shot straight into the glass, and slam the contents in one go. Another option is to pour the shot into the beer, keeping the shot glass out of your pint, or just consume the two by drinking the shot and chasing it with the beer. The fun part is to try to drink it all in one go, slam the glass (or glasses) down, and gasp for air.

Alternatively, drink your boilermaker like Maddie does in "Blonde on Blonde"—sip the shot of whiskey and then drink the glass of beer.

Choose your own adventure and enjoy the buzz!

The Rita

The Rita is inspired by the French 75, a classic American-style cocktail invented in Harry's New York Bar in Paris during World War I. In France, it is known simply as a soixante quinze, which translates to the number seventy-five in French. The combination was said to be so strong that it felt like being shelled by the powerful French 75mm field gun. This was a popular 1940s cocktail that would have been served in nightclubs like the Flamingo Cove in "The Dream Sequence Always Rings Twice," Season 2, Episode 4. This cocktail is sweet, sour, and strong, just like the character of Rita.

> 1 ounce gin
> 1/2 ounce freshly squeezed lemon juice
> 1/2 ounce simple syrup
> 3 ounces champagne
> Garnish: lemon twist

Add the gin, lemon juice, and simple syrup to a cocktail shaker filled with ice. Shake until well chilled, around thirty seconds. Strain into a champagne coupe (or flute) glass. Top with the champagne and garnish with the lemon twist.

The Zach

The Zach is inspired by a classic Negroni, an American-style cocktail that became popular in Italy in the 1940s. This cocktail would undoubtedly have been served in nightclubs like the Flamingo Cove in season two's "The Dream Sequence Always Rings Twice." The filmmaker and director Orson Welles famously enjoyed drinking Negronis while working in Rome on the movie *Cagliostro* in 1947 "the bitters are excellent for your liver, the gin is bad for you—they balance each other." This cocktail is a little sweet and a little sexy, with a hint of bitterness, just like the character of Zach.

    1 ounce gin
    1 ounce Campari
    1 ounce sweet vermouth
    Garnish: orange peel

Add the gin, Campari, and sweet vermouth to a mixing glass filled with ice and stir until well chilled. Strain into a lowball glass filled with ice cubes (alternatively, a single, large, perfect ice cube would be perfect here). Garnish with the orange peel.

Vicious Virgin

David: "A little free advice—never order a drink called a vicious virgin. At least don't order five of them in a row."
From "Big Man on Mulberry Street," Season 3, Episode 6

A vicious virgin is a tiki-inspired cocktail featuring rum and fruit juice, typically served in an old fashioned-style cocktail glass with crushed ice.

The enigmatic world traveler and adventurer Donn Beach is credited with inventing this cocktail at his Don the Beachcomber bar in Hollywood. This cocktail packs a punch! It's no wonder David woke up on the floor of a bar with a cop taking his pulse after five of these!

1 ounce light rum
1/2 ounce dark rum
1/2 ounce Cointreau
3/4 ounce freshly squeezed lime juice
1/2 ounce Falernum liqueur
Splash of grenadine
Lime wedge and maraschino cherry to garnish

Fill a cocktail shaker with ice. Add the rum, Cointreau, lime juice, Falernum, and grenadine. Shake well.

Strain into an old fashioned-style glass (or a tiki mug!) filled with crushed ice. Garnish with a lime wedge and a cherry.

Taming of the Shrewdriver

"Atomic Shakespeare," Season 4, Episode 7, is based on William Shakespeare's *The Taming of the Shrew*. As a play on words—minus the iambic pentameter—here is a recipe for a fun cocktail called a taming of the shrewdriver.

   1 1/2 ounces vodka
   1/2 ounce Cointreau
   6 ounces orange juice
   2 ounces grapefruit, peach, or Bellini flavored sparkling water

Add the orange juice, vodka, and Cointreau to a highball glass. Top with the sparkling water. Stir well.
   Add ice cubes and serve.

Martini

Maddie: "Another."
Bartender: "You wanna talk about it?"
Maddie: "No, I definitely want another."
Bartender: "Now why is a beautiful lady like yourself sitting alone in a bar ordering double martinis?"
From "It's a Wonderful Job," Season 3, Episode 8

In season three's "It's a Wonderful Job," Maddie orders two martinis at the bar where she meets her guardian angel. And in season five's "Lunar Eclipse," Annie's husband, Mark, orders a martini for himself and David—David opts for a beer instead, and Mark makes a toast to his wife—and her lover.

A martini is a classic cocktail made with gin (or vodka) and dry vermouth. For a dirty martini, you can add olive brine to this mix.

> 2 ounces high quality gin (or vodka for a vodka martini)
> 1 ounce dry vermouth (if you prefer a dry martini, add half an ounce)
> For a dirty martini: 2 teaspoons olive brine
> Garnish: strip of lemon peel or 2 cocktail olives

Fill a cocktail shaker with ice and add the gin (or vodka), vermouth, and, if using, olive brine. Shake until ice cold, thirty to forty-five seconds.

Strain into a martini glass and garnish with either a strip of lemon peel or a pick with cocktail olives.

Cranberry Syringe Cocktail

Inspired by "Poltergeist III, Dipesto Nothing," Season 3, Episode 10. In season three's "Poltergeist III, Dipesto Nothing," Miss Dipesto takes a case on by herself and ends up in the middle of a scary situation with a house full of terrified people, including a clairvoyant and a crazy doctor! Bert comes to her rescue, but Agnes ends up being chased by the doctor, who tries to kill her with a hypodermic needle filled with poison! This cocktail is a homage to that scene.

 4 ounces chilled lemon-lime soda
 1/2 ounce cranberry juice
 1/2 ounce vodka

Fill a highball glass halfway with chilled soda. Mix the cranberry juice and vodka together in a separate glass and draw into the syringe. Place the vodka-and-cranberry-juice-filled syringe into the soda. To drink, either shoot the syringe directly into your mouth and chase it with the soda or inject the shot into the glass of soda, stir, and enjoy as a cocktail.

White Wine Spritzer

Maddie: "I'll have a club soda. No, a white wine spritzer. No, make that a boilermaker." From "Blonde on Blonde," Season 3, Episode 11

In season three's "Blonde on Blonde," Maddie is feeling lonely and goes to the Los Angeles nightclub Metropolis to meet someone. When the bartender asks her what she wants to drink, she first orders a club soda with lime, then changes her order to a white wine spritzer. After looking at all the men ogling her at the bar, she decides she needs something stronger—a boilermaker. But I like to think that what Maddie really wanted to order was this white wine spritzer—it is a very Maddie Hayes drink.

4 ounces chilled white wine
1 ounce club soda
Garnish: Lemon slice

Fill a wine glass with crushed ice. Pour in the chilled white wine and top with the club soda. Garnish with a lemon slice.

Double Shot of My Baby's Love

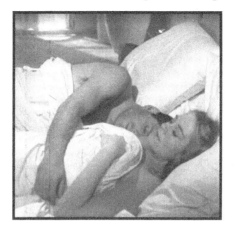

David comes into the office happy the morning after the night before! He sings "Double Shot of My Baby's Love" by the Swingin' Medallions: "To Heiress Human," Season 3, Episode 15

This cocktail is inspired by Maddie and David's "Big Bang" evening and the song a very happy David sings when he comes into the office the following morning in the season four finale "To Heiress Human." It contains a double shot of liquor—coconut rum and peach schnapps-and is both potent and sweet, just like David's love for Maddie.

2 ounces cranberry juice
1 ounce peach schnapps
1 1/2 ounces coconut rum
Garnish: 1 strawberry

Add all the ingredients to a cocktail shaker filled with ice. Shake for thirty seconds, until well chilled. Pour into a chilled martini or coupe glass. Garnish with a strawberry slice.

Shiksa Sour

In "Come Back, Little Shiksa," Season 4, Episode 2, David learns that Maddie has left LA to stay with her parents in Chicago. In a fit of rage, he intentionally crashes the BMW multiple times in the Blue Moon parking garage. This cocktail is the perfect antidote to a stressful day like the one David and Maddie have both had!

 2 ounces apricot nectar
 1 1/2 ounces gin
 1/2 ounce freshly squeezed lemon juice
 1/2 ounce simple syrup
 3 drops Angostura bitters
 Garnish: lemon slice

Fill a cocktail shaker with ice and add the apricot nectar, gin, lemon juice, simple syrup, and bitters. Shake for thirty seconds, until well chilled. Serve immediately in a coupe glass garnished with a lemon slice.

Margarita

Rita: "How about a margarita?" David: "Por qué no?" (Spanish for "Why not?") David (always the bartender at heart) mixes some in her blender. From "A Tale in Two Cities," Season 4, Episode 4

There are several references to margaritas in *Moonlighting*, including season four's "A Tale in Two Cities" and season five's "I See England, I See France, I See Maddie's Netherworld," "When Girls Collide," and "Eine Kleine Nacht Murder".

This recipe is for a margarita on the rocks with an option for making frozen margaritas like David does in "A Tale in Two Cities." The simple syrup used here is optional—not necessary if you are using a higher-end gold tequila but recommended for other tequilas!

```
4 ounces high-quality gold tequila
2 ounces triple sec or Cointreau
1 1/2 ounces freshly squeezed lime juice
1/2 ounce simple syrup (optional)
Garnish: lime wedges and coarse salt
```

Optional: Run a lime wedge around the rim of a margarita glass and dip the rim in salt. Set aside. For an on-the-rocks margarita: add ice to a cocktail shaker and pour in the tequila, triple sec, and lime juice. Shake until chilled, about thirty seconds. Fill the glass with ice and strain the margarita into the glass. Garnish with a lime wedge and serve. For a frozen margarita: add the mixture to a blender with one cup of crushed ice and blend until frosty. Serve in a margarita glass.

The Ingrid

David: "North Pole, Santa Speaking, Ho Ho Ho! Sure, I'm sure this is Santa Claus. Who is this? Ingrid! And how old are you, Ingrid? 23?! Really!? So tell me, Ingrid, you been good? You been good a lot?"
From "'Twas The Episode Before Christmas," Season 2, Episode 10

You Been Good?

4 ounces apple juice
1 ounce orange juice
1 ounce gingerbread simple syrup
Garnish: 1 cinnamon stick

Would You Like to Be Great?

3 ounces whiskey or bourbon
1 ounce Cointreau
1 ounce orange juice
2 dashes orange bitters
1 ounce gingerbread simple syrup
Garnish: 1 cinnamon stick

To make the gingerbread simple syrup, add the brown sugar, water, ground cinnamon, and ground ginger to a saucepan. Heat over medium heat for five minutes or until the sugar is melted. Remove from heat and add the vanilla extract. Cool to room temperature. Mixture can be stored in the fridge for up to one month.

For the cocktail, add all ingredients to a shaker filled with ice. Shake for thirty seconds or until well chilled. Strain into a lowball glass filled with ice. Garnish with a cinnamon stick.

Santa's Hotline

David: "Santa's Hotline, North Pole, Santa Speaking! Ho Ho Ho!""
From "'Twas The Episode Before Christmas," Season 2, Episode 10

2 ounces peppermint vodka
1 ounce Bailey's Irish Cream
1 ounce half and half
Garnish: 1 candy cane and white and red sanding sugar (or crushed candy cane)

Add all ingredients to a shaker filled with ice. Shake for 30 seconds or until well chilled.

Dip the rim of a martini glass in water. Add sanding sugar or crushed peppermint candy to a plate. Run the rim of the glass through the sugar to decorate.

Strain into the prepared martini glass and garnish with a candy cane.

Cool Hand Dave

In "Cool Hand Dave Parts 1 and 2," Season 4, Episodes 5 and 6, David and Bert are talking about David's "nineteen innings" with Rita the night before, and David is drinking chocolate milk, his favorite non-alcoholic beverage. Bert is just about to spill the beans that Maddie is pregnant.

This cocktail is in honor of David Addison and his love of chocolate milk. It is a variation of a classic White Russian, using chocolate milk instead of the usual cream.

    2 ounces vodka
    1 ounce Kahlua
    3 ounces whole milk
    3 teaspoons dark chocolate syrup

Fill a cocktail shaker with ice and add the vodka, Kahlua, milk, and chocolate syrup. Shake until well mixed and icy cold, around thirty seconds. Pour into a lowball glass filled with ice cubes.

Golden Wine Cooler

David: "I'm pretty sure I can tell you everything there is to know about Bachelor Number 2."
Bert: "But you've never met him."
David: "You know the kind of guy Ms. Hayes goes for. She's a bone structure freak. Look at Sam. Broad shoulders, slim waist, trim hips. Think Clint Eastwood. Think of that guy that does those cooler commercials. He's gonna be a big hunk or a slab of something. It's all in the packaging."
From "Maddie Hayes Got Married," Season 4, Episode 12

This recipe is inspired by the famous Seagram's wine coolers popular in the 1980s, featuring print and television ads with Bruce Willis, and mentioned in a tongue-in-cheek way in "Maddie Hayes Got Married." As the famous slogan goes: it's wet and it's dry!

> 4 ounces dry chardonnay
> 3 ounces ginger ale
> 1 ounce Grand Marnier

Fill a wine glass with crushed ice. Add the chardonnay, Grand Marnier, and ginger ale. Stir to combine.

Sangria

David: "Well that's enough business for this morning. Let's go to lunch. I'm buying. The last thing I remember is bobbing for lemon wedges in a vat of sangria." From "The Color of Maddie," Season 5, Episode 3

    1 medium green apple, cored and chopped into small pieces
    1 medium red apple, cored and chopped into small pieces
    1 medium seedless orange, sliced into small pieces
    2 lemons, sliced into small pieces
    3 tablespoons sugar
    1 bottle dry red wine
    3/4 cup orange juice
    1/3 cup brandy

Add the apples, oranges, lemons, and sugar to a large pitcher and muddle with a wooden spoon for one minute. Add the orange juice, brandy, and red wine and stir to incorporate.

Chill in the refrigerator until ready to serve. Serve in wine glasses, with or without ice.

Best served the same day it is made but can be stored in the refrigerator for up to forty-eight hours. Serves six.

–CHAPTER 2–
Appetizers & First Courses

Moonlighting is filled with references to appetizers and starters. From the goat cheese salads that the waiter keeps dropping in "The Lady in the Iron Mask" to the rumaki that Virginia Hayes serves to her cocktail party guests in "A Tale in Two Cities," appetizers, soups, salads, and other starters are referenced throughout the series.

We start with La Serre, a high-end Los Angeles restaurant in the San Fernando Valley that opened in 1974. It is famous in the *Moonlighting* metaverse as the location of Glenn Gordon Caron and Jay Daniel's first meeting with Cybill Shepherd in 1984 to discuss the part of Maddie Hayes in *Moonlighting*—and the rest, as they say, is kismet.

La Serre served stylish (and expensive) French cuisine and was known for both excellent service and delicious food. It was a favorite for power lunches because of the privacy of the rooms and attracted both Hollywood elite and upscale business people. It was an upscale Los Angeles favorite until it closed its doors in 1991. For more information about La Serre, visit the "*Moonlighting* Restaurants & Nightclubs: A History" section of this book.

French Onion Soup

Inspired by La Serre 12969 Ventura Boulevard
Studio City, Los Angeles, California (Closed in 1991)

This recipe is inspired by the famous French onion soup served at La Serre.

> 3 pounds sweet yellow onions, halved and sliced very thin
> 1 stick unsalted butter
> 2 cups dry white wine
> 8 cups beef broth
> 2 teaspoons finely chopped fresh thyme
> Salt and Pepper, to taste
> 8 ounces Gruyère(or Swiss) cheese, shredded
> 4 ounces fresh parmesan, grated
> 1 small French baguette, sliced into cubes

In a large stockpot on medium high heat, melt the butter and sauté the onions for twenty minutes, until the onions caramelize. Deglaze the pan with the white wine and simmer uncovered for five minutes. Add the beef broth and thyme and simmer for another twenty minutes.

Meanwhile, preheat the broiler. Add the bread cubes to four oven proof soup crocks. When the soup is finished, ladle the soup over the bread cubes and top the soup with the grated cheeses. Broil until the cheese is melted and browned all over. Serve immediately. Serves four.

Goat Cheese Salad with Balsamic Vinaigrette

One of the most iconic *Moonlighting* chase scenes takes place in season two's "The Lady in the Iron Mask," Season 2, Episode 2. David; Maddie; the lady in the iron mask, Barbara Wylie; and her husband, Benjamin Wylie are all dressed identically and chasing one another through the Ambassador Hotel in Los Angeles with the famous "William Tell Overture" playing in the background. In the middle of this chase, they run through the kitchen and banquet room and keep knocking over the same poor waiter (a very young C. Thomas Howell), who keeps trying to serve food to the patrons dining there. On his tray, he is serving a very popular 1980s starter, a goat cheese salad.

8 cups mixed baby greens
1/2 cup chopped toasted walnuts
1 small log goat cheese, crumbled
1 small shallot, finely minced
1 tablespoon balsamic vinegar
2 teaspoons Dijon mustard
3 tablespoons extra-virgin olive oil
1/4 teaspoon kosher salt
Freshly ground black pepper

In a small bowl, whisk together the shallot, vinegar, mustard, salt, and pepper. Gradually whisk in the olive oil to make a creamy dressing. Toss the dressing with the salad greens and place greens on four salad plates. Top with the goat cheese and walnuts. Serves four.

Chicken Lickin' Nuggets

Maddie: "We could have been in charge of all of the security for all of the Chicken Lickin' stores in all of California. I had Mr. Lickin' eating out of my hand." . . .
David: "Well—haven't you ever wondered whatever happened to the eyes, the beaks, and the feet?
From "Money Talks, Maddie Walks," Season 2, Episode 3

Chicken nuggets were a new menu item in restaurants across the country in the early 1980s, and they were an instant hit. McDonald's introduced Chicken McNuggets in 1983, and they have remained popular ever since. This recipe is inspired by the Chicken Lickin' nuggets and are, thankfully, eye, beak, and feet free!

3 boneless, skinless chicken breasts, cut into 1-inch pieces
1 cup milk
1 cup dill pickle juice
1 large egg, beaten
1 cup all-purpose flour
1 tablespoon powdered sugar
1 teaspoon paprika
1 teaspoon salt
1 teaspoon pepper
Canola or peanut oil, for frying

Brine the chicken by combining it with the pickle juice in a medium bowl. Cover and refrigerate overnight. The next day, remove the chicken from the refrigerator and drain.

In a small bowl, whisk together the egg and milk. Pour this mixture over the chicken pieces and combine well. In a large ziplock bag, combine the dry ingredients. Drain the excess milk off of the chicken and add to the bag of dry ingredients. Seal the bag and shake well to thoroughly coat the chicken.

Heat the oil in a large, heavy pan over medium heat (you can also use a fryer). Working in batches, add the chicken to the hot oil and cook until golden brown and crispy, around four to five minutes. Move the cooked chicken nuggets to a plate lined with paper towels.

The Wobblies' Stuffed Mushrooms

Maddie (to the Wobblies): "You're all fungi!!"
From "My Fair David," Season 2, Episode 5

In season two's "My Fair David," Maddie and David make a bet that he can't be a mature adult for a week. Agnes and the Wobblies are upset that Maddie has "De-Daved" David. Maddie admits she misses the old David but says she can tell jokes too. When they don't laugh at her jokes, Maddie tells the Wobblies they are all fungi!

1 1/2 cups boiling water
1 6-ounce package Stove Top Chicken Stuffing Mix
2 pounds fresh white button mushrooms—about 40 mushrooms
2 tablespoons unsalted butter
2 cloves garlic, minced
1 10-ounce box frozen chopped spinach, thawed
1 cup shredded mozzarella cheese
1 cup grated parmesan cheese

Preheat the oven to 400 degrees. Drain the thawed spinach. Squeeze well to get out all of the water. Remove dirt from mushrooms and remove stems. Finely chop stems.

In a skillet on medium heat, melt the butter. Add the chopped mushroom stems and garlic. Cook for five minutes, stirring occasionally, until tender and lightly browned.

In a large bowl, add boiling water to the stuffing mix and stir until moistened. Add the mushroom stem and garlic mixture, drained spinach, mozzarella, and parmesan. Mix well.

Place the mushroom caps on a baking sheet. Fill each mushroom cap with the stuffing mixture.

Bake for twenty minutes. Serve warm or at room temperature.

Leprechaun Lucky Rainbow Fruit Tray

This is a fun snack tray for St. Patrick's Day—or your "Somewhere Under the Rainbow," Season 2, Episode 7, watch party! It features a mix of fruit and candies or cheeses and is a hit with kids and adults alike.

> 1 bag individually gold-wrapped chocolate caramel candies or chocolate coins
> 1 small container vanilla meringues OR 1 large package miniature round cheeses, unwrapped and red wax removed
> 1 quart strawberries, hulled and sliced
> 1 cantaloupe, cut into cubes
> 1 fresh pineapple, cut into cubes
> 1 bunch green grapes
> 1 pint blueberries

On a large serving platter, assemble the fruits into the shape of a rainbow, using the red-orange-yellow-green-blue-violet rainbow order.

Add the meringues or miniature cheeses as a cloud option at the end of each side of your fruit rainbow.

Add the chocolates to a ramekin or small pot and place in between the meringue clouds.

David's Popcorn

In season two's "The Bride of Tupperman," Season 2, Episode 11, David enjoys a large bowl of popcorn in his office while watching *The Bride of Frankenstein*. This stovetop popcorn recipe is inspired by this scene.

> 2 tablespoons vegetable oil
> 1/2 cup popcorn kernels
> 1/4 cup melted butter
> Salt, to taste

Preheat the vegetable oil in a large heavy stockpot over medium-high heat. Add a couple of test kernels. When these test kernels pop, add the remainder of the popcorn. Cover the pot with a lid and reduce heat to medium. Cook until the popping noises subside. Be sure not to let the popcorn burn! Pour into a large serving bowl and stir in melted butter and add salt to taste. Serve immediately.

Potato Skins

In "Sleep Talkin' Guy," Season 2, Episode 16, David has been working with Toby, a prostitute, who has been feeding him information to help solve crimes, making David a police darling and local celebrity. David meets Toby at a bar for happy hour, and the Sleep Talkin' Guy, Jerry, is there with her. Chaos ensues when Maddie shows up and Jerry realizes that David — who he thought was Toby's brother — is actually David Addison. A food fight erupts, and David and some of the other bar patrons throw platters of happy hours appetizers at one another. One of these platters is potato skins — a quintessential eighties appetizer!

8 small russet potatoes (about 2 1/2 pounds), washed well
4 tablespoons vegetable oil
2 tablespoons butter
Kosher salt, to taste
2 cups grated sharp cheddar cheese
8 slices bacon, cooked until crispy and chopped
1/2 cup sour cream
3 green onions or a small bunch of chives, finely chopped

Preheat the oven to 400 degrees. Rub the outside of the potatoes with two tablespoons of vegetable oil until moistened. Place the potatoes on a baking sheet and bake until the potatoes are tender and the skin is crisp, about forty-five minutes. Allow the potatoes to cool for about fifteen minutes until cool enough to handle. Cut the potatoes in half lengthwise and scoop insides out, leaving a little bit of potato in the skins. (You can save the potato insides for another purpose, like soup, or just discard.)

In a saucepan, melt the butter with the remaining two tablespoons vegetable oil. Brush the mixture on the insides and outsides of the potato skins. Sprinkle lightly with salt and pepper. Return the potato skins to the baking sheet and bake until golden brown and crispy, about twenty minutes. Remove the potato skins from the oven and sprinkle with the cheddar and bacon. Return to the oven again to allow the cheese to melt, about five minutes longer.

Serve immediately topped with sour cream and green onions or chives.

Camille's Charcuterie

In the season two finale, "Camille", Season 2, Episode 18, the con artist Camille — played by Whoopi Goldberg — enjoys a charcuterie tray, and other goodies, in her hotel room. David and Maddie come to her room to try to persuade her to join Blue Moon as an investigator.

This charcuterie board is inspired by this episode — for a special 1980s nostalgic touch, serve with fancy toothpicks like Camille's board has!

    8 ounces hard salami
    8 ounces prosciutto
    8 ounces cheddar cheese, cut into cubes
    8 ounces Gouda cheese, cut into cubes
    8 ounces Swiss cheese, cut into cubes
    1 package table water crackers
    1/2 cup roasted almonds
    2 cups grapes
    2 apples, sliced

On a medium cheese board or platter, arrange the cheeses and meats. Add the almonds to a small bowl and place on the cheese board. Add the fresh fruit and crackers. Serve and enjoy!

Seven-Layer Dip

In the season-three premiere, "The Son Also Rises," Season 3, Episode 1, the Blue Moon employees are returning to the office after a two-week vacation. David went to Mexico and comes back wearing a sombrero and poncho and leads the group in singing "La Bamba," dancing, and hitting a piñata. He also has a special gift for Maddie: maracas.

This dip is inspired by David's Mexican vacation. Seven-layer dip was one of the most popular party appetizers of the 1980s and remains popular today.

1 16-ounce can refried pinto beans
1 4-ounce can diced green chiles
1 4-ounce can sliced black olives
1 cup shredded cheddar cheese
1 cup shredded Monterey Jack cheese
1 cup sour cream
1 cup guacamole
(store bought is fine or you can make your own)
1 cup pico de gallo
(store bought is fine or you can make your own)
Hot sauce and chili powder, to taste
Tortilla chips, for dipping

In a small saucepan, heat the refried beans on medium-low heat. Add the hot sauce and chili powder, to taste. Add the green chiles and stir well. Assemble the 7 layers in a pie plate or glass bowl in the following order:

1. Refried beans
2. Cheddar cheese
3. Sour cream
4. Guacamole
5. Monterey Jack cheese
6. Black Olives
7. Pico de Gallo

Serve immediately with tortilla chips for dipping.

Brown Sugar Bacon Appetizers

Maddie: "You are a vile unevolved swine."
David: "Yes I am."
Maddie: "You don't deserve to belly up to the same trough with the rest of the pigs. You give bacon a bad name."
From "All Creatures Great . . . and Not So Great," Season 3, Episode 5

This bacon appetizer is inspired by this exchange between Maddie and David in "All Creatures Great . . . and Not So Great." And who can forget David's pig earring in "Witness for the Execution"?

1 package bacon
1 sleeve club-style crackers
3/4 cup brown sugar

Preheat the oven to 250 degrees. Lay the crackers on a large rack over a half-sheet baking pan. Scoop a teaspoon of brown sugar onto each cracker.

Cut the slices of bacon from the package in half. Carefully wrap each brown-sugar-covered cracker with one half slice of bacon, completely covering the cracker. It should fit snugly around the cracker but not be pulled too tight. Place the bacon-wrapped crackers onto the rack and bake for about two hours. Serve immediately or at room temperature.

Virginia Hayes's Marinated Vegetable Salad

At the beginning of season four's "Take a Left at the Altar," Season 4, Episode 3, Alex and Virginia Hayes are preparing a vegetable salad and talking about what's going on with Maddie—why she's been home for so long, why she doesn't want to go anywhere or see anyone, and why she hasn't called her office or her friends.

I recognized this salad immediately because it's one my own mom used to make for her bridge luncheons in the 1970s and 1980s. This is a great recipe that keeps well in the fridge for a couple of days and is equally nice for a lunch with friends or a brown-bag-style lunch at work.

For the salad:
1 large yellow bell pepper, sliced into strips
3 carrots, peeled and sliced into thin rounds
1 cup cauliflower florets
1 cup broccoli florets
1 cup fresh green beans, cut into 1-inch pieces
1 cup white button mushrooms, sliced
5 green onions, sliced

For the dressing:
1 teaspoon brown mustard
1/2 teaspoon garlic salt
1/2 teaspoon salt
1/2 teaspoon black pepper
1/4 teaspoon red pepper flakes
1 teaspoon sugar
1 teaspoons Worcestershire sauce
3-4 drops hot sauce
1/4 cup apple cider vinegar
3/4 cup extra-virgin olive oil

Blanch all of the vegetables except for the mushrooms and green onions in boiling water for three to four minutes. Drain, rinse, and cover with ice cubes to stop the cooking process. Drain.

Combine the dry salad ingredients in a large measuring cup. Add the Worcestershire sauce, vinegar, and hot sauce and whisk until well mixed. Drizzle in the olive oil, whisking constantly, until dressing comes together.

Combine all the vegetables in a large bowl and pour the dressing over them. Refrigerate for at least four hours or overnight. Drain before serving.

Virginia Hayes's Rumaki

Virginia: "I know, I'll order a nice platter of petit fours."
Alex: "Honey, this is not a croquet match. It's a cocktail party. Let's have some hot hors d'oeuvres."
Virginia: "Fine, so I'll make some rumaki."
Alex: "Well I don't have to eat them. I'll get the booze."
From "A Tale in Two Cities," Season 4, Episode 4

In "A Tale in Two Cities," Alex and Virginia decide to throw a cocktail party to coax Maddie out of her childhood bedroom to visit with them and their friends. Virginia decides to make rumaki, which is clearly not Alex's favorite appetizer—and judging by its reception at the cocktail party (one guest intentionally drops one on the floor and kicks it under a coffee table), Alex isn't the only one!

Rumaki were a hugely popular appetizer from the 1960s through the 1980s. Virginia Hayes's version is made with chicken livers, but another version substitutes water chestnuts for the chicken livers. This recipe is for the latter.

1 pound bacon
8 ounces whole water chestnuts, canned
1/4 cup soy sauce
1 1/2 cups light brown sugar
3/4 cup ketchup
1 tablespoon apple cider vinegar
1 tablespoon sugar

Preheat the oven to 350 degrees.

Cut bacon in half crosswise and wrap each water chestnut with a piece of bacon. Secure with a toothpick. Line a half-sheet pan with parchment and add the prepared water chestnuts in rows. Bake for twenty-five minutes and drain the grease.

Meanwhile, combine the soy sauce, light brown sugar, ketchup, sugar, and vinegar. Toss the prepared water chestnuts in sauce and return to the baking sheet. Bake for twenty minutes or until glaze is set.

Serve warm.

Virginia Hayes's Spinach Dip & Veggies

Virginia and Alex Hayes serve spinach dip and veggies at their cocktail party. They serve theirs with Keebler Toasteds crackers, but for a little extra 1980s flair, I recommend serving the dip in a bread bowl with the veggies alongside!

1 box frozen chopped spinach, defrosted and squeezed dry
1 16-ounce container sour cream
1 cup mayonnaise
1 package vegetable soup mix
1 can water chestnuts, drained and chopped
3 green onions, finely chopped
1 round loaf of Hawaiian bread
Sliced veggies, for serving: carrots, broccoli, red bell pepper, cucumbers

Combine all the ingredients in a bowl and mix well. Chill for two hours.

To serve, hollow out the round loaf of bread. Cut the hollowed-out pieces of bread into cubes. Add dip to the bread bowl. Serve with the bread cubes and veggies on the side.

Agnes and MacGillicudy's Cocktail Franks

MacGillicuddy: "Agnes, thanks for being here. Excuse me while I procure some more cocktail franks."
Agnes (later, to Bert): "I am exercising my constitutional right for free association by having cocktail franks with whomever I please."
From "A Tale in Two Cities," Season 4, Episode 4

In "A Tale in Two Cities," Agnes and MacGillicuddy go out for happy hour to a bar named Cahoots and enjoy cocktail franks with their cocktails at the bar. MacGillicudy's wife just left him, and Agnes is being a good friend to him. Bert shows up and feels otherwise. This recipe is inspired by this scene.

- 1 12-ounce bottle barbecue sauce
- 1 8-ounce jar grape jelly
- 2 14-ounce packages miniature smoked sausages

In a slow cooker, combine the barbecue sauce and the grape jelly. Stir in the cocktail franks. Cook on high until heated through, about two to three hours. Serve warm with cocktail picks.

Shrimp Cocktail

Shrimp cocktail is featured in two episodes of *Moonlighting*. In "Sleep Talkin' Guy," Season 2, Episode 16, Toby and Jerry (the prostitute and sleep talker) have shrimp cocktail in their hotel room. And in "Tracks of My Tears," Season 4, Episode 10, Maddie has a shrimp cocktail on the train in the dining car with Walter Bishop.

This recipe features roasted shrimp instead of the usual steamed or boiled ones and a simple homemade cocktail sauce

For the roasted shrimp:
2 pounds shrimp, peeled and deveined, tails on
1 tablespoon extra-virgin olive oil
1/2 teaspoon kosher salt
1/2 teaspoon black pepper

For the cocktail sauce:
1/2 cup chili sauce
1/2 cup ketchup
3 tablespoons horseradish sauce
1 teaspoon Worcestershire sauce
Fresh lemon wedges, for serving

Preheat the oven to 400 degrees. Place the shrimp on a half sheet pan and toss with the olive oil, salt, and pepper. Roast for ten minutes until just pink and cooked through. Set aside to cool.

Combine the sauce ingredients in a bowl and mix well.

Serve the shrimp in shrimp cocktail glasses with dollops of sauce in the center and lemon wedges on the side.

California Rolls

In "Plastic Fantastic Lovers," Season 5, Episode 4, David receives a video from a potential client. He and Maddie go into his office to play the video, and when Maddie starts the VCR, there is already a tape in there called *Hot Sushi Girls*, and it begins to play. This conversation ensues:

Maddie: "How could she eat raw fish?"

David: "It's red snapper. An acquired taste."

Los Angeles was a leader in the trendsetting cuisine of sushi in the 1980s. California rolls, which contain cucumber, avocado, and imitation crab meat, were a popular 1980s sushi order, and remain popular today. The earliest mention in print of a California roll was in the *Los Angeles Times* on November 25, 1979, and this article attributes its invention to a Los Angeles-based chef named Ken Seusa at Kin Jo Sushi in Hollywood.

2 1/4 cups water
1 1/2 cups sushi rice
2 tablespoons seasoned rice wine vinegar
1 teaspoon salt
1 teaspoon sugar
1 large ripe avocado

1/2 English cucumber
8 ounces imitation crab (get the logs/leg style, not chunks)
4 sheets toasted nori seaweed
Soy sauce, wasabi, and pickled ginger, for serving

Rinse the rice well in a colander. In a medium saucepan, add the rice and the water. Bring to a boil. Once boiling, put on the lid and reduce the heat to low. Cook for twenty minutes. When the rice is done, add the sugar, salt, and vinegar. Mix well and set aside to cool thoroughly. Thinly slice the avocado, and slice the cucumber into long, thin strips.

Lay the shiny side of a sheet of nori down onto a sushi mat. Transfer a cup of prepared rice to the center of the nori sheet. With wet fingers, spread the rice out across the length and width of the seaweed. Add a line of the avocado, the crab, and the cucumber on top of the rice. Roll the sushi roll up using the sushi mat as a guide. Remove from the mat and cut into eight pieces. Repeat with the other three sheets of nori—this recipe makes four full California rolls. Serve with soy sauce, wasabi, and pickled ginger.

Viola Antipasto Salad

In "In 'N Outlaws," Season 5, Episode 11, Bert attends the Viola family reunion and serves as the event's videographer. He is upset that Agnes is sequestered in a locked jury and cannot attend the event with him. At the event, there is a large banner that reads, "Welcome Violas! Veni Vidi Violi!" A large antipasto platter is one of the many Italian food items served at this colorful event!

This recipe is for a vegetable-filled antipasto salad that would be right at home at a Viola family gathering!

3 cups asparagus, cut into 2-inch pieces
3 cups quartered button mushrooms
1 cup red bell pepper strips
1 cup pitted large black olives
8 ounces mozzarella cheese, cubed
1 14-ounce can quartered artichoke hearts, drained
1 12-ounce jar sliced pepperoncini peppers, drained

1/3 cup apple cider vinegar
1/4 cup chopped Italian parsley
1/4 cup extra-virgin olive oil
1 teaspoon sugar
1/4 teaspoon salt
1/4 teaspoon black pepper
2 teaspoons Italian seasoning
3 fresh garlic cloves, finely minced

Blanch the asparagus in boiling water for two minutes. Drain and plunge into ice water. Drain well.

Whisk the vinegar, sugar, salt, pepper, Italian seasoning, garlic, and chopped parsley in a small bowl.

Combine the vegetables and mozzarella in a large bowl. Pour the dressing over the vegetables and toss to coat. Cover and marinate in the refrigerator for two to three hours. Serve cold or at room temperature.

–CHAPTER 3–
MAIN DISHES

Moonlighting contains many scenes in which Maddie and David dine out with clients, family members, dates, and friends. Maddie's date with "Dr. Face Fixer" at the Westin Bonaventure in the pilot, the epic food fight at the Millennium Biltmore in "The Murder's in the Mail," dinner at Adriano's with David's brother Richie in "Brother, Can You Spare a Blonde?," dinner with Alex and Virginia Hayes at Le Bel Age in "Every Daughter's Father Is a Virgin," and David interrupting Maddie and Sam's dinner in "Sam and Dave" are all memorable and pivotal scenes in *Moonlighting* involving meals out. The main dishes in this chapter are inspired by these *Moonlighting* moments.

Kung Pao Chicken

All *Moonlighting* fans will recognize Hong Kong Café from the show's opening credits for seasons one, two, and three. This recipe is inspired by this iconic Chinatown restaurant and club. For more information about the historic Hong Kong Café, see the "*Moonlighting* Restaurants & Nightclubs: A History" section of this book.

For the chicken and marinade:
1 pound boneless, skinless chicken thighs, thinly sliced
2 tablespoons cornstarch
2 tablespoons soy sauce
2 tablespoons mirin
2 tablespoons brown sugar

For the stir fry:
2 medium zucchini, cut into 1-inch cubes
1 medium red bell pepper, cut into 1-inch pieces
1 green bell pepper, cut into 1-inch pieces
1 medium yellow onion, cut into 1-inch pieces
3 green onions, chopped
1 cup unsalted dry roasted peanuts, chopped
3 garlic cloves, minced
1 tablespoon vegetable oil
2 tablespoons soy sauce
2 teaspoons sesame oil
1 teaspoon chili-garlic sauce (or to taste)
1/2 teaspoon black pepper

For the marinade: Slice the chicken into quarter-inch bite size pieces. Whisk the marinade ingredients in a large bowl and add the chicken. Marinate for at least thirty minutes and up to all day.

For the stir fry: chop the zucchini, peppers, onion, and garlic. Whisk together the soy sauce, sesame oil, chili-garlic sauce, and black pepper.

Heat a wok or large sauté pan over medium high heat. Add the vegetable oil. Add the chicken and cook until browned and slightly crispy, about four to five minutes. Remove from the pan. Add the vegetables and stir fry for another three to four minutes until crisp tender. Add the peanuts and stir fry for another minute. Stir in the chicken and the stir fry sauce and cook for another one to two minutes, until thick and well coated. Stir in the scallions. Serve warm with steamed white rice.

Serves four.

Baked Rock Lobster Tails

David: "Oh wow! Lobster! My favorite!"
From the Pilot, Season 1, Episode 1

David interrupts Maddie's date with the plastic surgeon at the Top of Five restaurant at the Westin Bonaventure Hotel in downtown Los Angeles. Maddie's date has ordered lobster and is wearing a lobster bib when he has a phone call "emergency," leaving David to sit with Maddie at their table.

2 8-ounce lobster tails (thawed if frozen)
1 large lemon
2 cloves garlic, finely minced
4 tablespoons unsalted butter (1/2 stick)
1/2 teaspoon kosher salt
1/4 cup fresh Italian parsley, chopped

If the lobster tails are frozen, place on a plate and refrigerate overnight to thaw. Preheat the oven to 425 degrees. Add enough water to an eight-by-eight baking dish to cover the bottom.

Using kitchen shears, butterfly the lobster tails by cutting through the softer shell on the bottom lengthwise. Pat the lobster tails dry. Using your fingers, gently pry the meat away from the shell on either side by working your thumb between the shell and the meat. This will make it easier to eat once the lobster is cooked.

Place the lobster tails flesh side up in a single layer in the baking dish. Cover the baking dish tightly with aluminum foil. Bake until the lobster meat is firm and cooked through and the internal temperature reaches 140 degrees. This will take about twenty-five minutes.

While the lobster is cooking, melt the butter in a small saucepan and add garlic and cook until fragrant but not browned, about thirty seconds. Add the juice of one lemon, salt, and parsley. Remove from heat and stir until combined. When the lobster is ready, transfer to serving plates and drizzle with the lemon garlic butter.

Serves two.

Fettuccine Alfredo

In "The Murder's in the Mail," Season 1, Episode 6, Maddie and David attempt to diffuse a major diplomatic incident. They try to get into the banquet by saying, "We're looking for a man with a mole on his nose," to no avail. They dress up as a waiter and waitress, and a crazy food fight breaks out. The entrée being served—and thrown!—is fettuccine Alfredo. This simple and delicious recipe is inspired by this episode—definitely better eaten than thrown!

This banquet scene was filmed in the Tiffany Room of the Millennium Biltmore Hotel, located at 506 South Grand Avenue in Los Angeles. It's still open, and you can visit today!

1 16-ounce package fettuccine
1 stick unsalted butter
1 cup heavy cream
2 cups freshly grated parmesan cheese
Salt and pepper, to taste

Cook the pasta according to package directions. In a large skillet, melt the butter and add the cream. Warm but do not boil. Season to taste with salt and freshly ground black pepper. Turn off the heat and add one cup of the grated parmesan cheese and stir to combine.

Drain the pasta, reserving one-half cup pasta water. Add the pasta to the butter, cream, and cheese mixture. Toss to combine. Add the remaining parmesan and toss again. Thin with a little of the reserved pasta water if the pasta-and-sauce mixture is too thick. Serve immediately. Makes four main-course servings.

Blackened Redfish

In "The Bride of Tupperman," Season 2, Episode 11, David discovers that Maddie's Friday night date has canceled—he has to go to a wedding (his own!)—so he asks her if she wants to do something with him that night. This dialogue ensues:

> David: "Dinner. Hard to screw up. We both like to eat. This time you choose. Anywhere you wanna go."
> Maddie: "Well, there is this new restaurant a couple of blocks away. Supposed to have wonderful seafood."
> David (grimaces): "Seafood?!"

Chef Paul Prudhomme was responsible for popularizing Cajun cuisine—and in particular blackened redfish—in the 1980s. His bestselling cookbook "Paul Prudhomme's Louisiana Kitchen" was published in 1984, bringing Cajun cuisine recipes to the home cook. You could also buy his Cajun seasoning in spice aisles in the grocery store beginning in the 1980s.

Blackened redfish was **THE** seafood dish of the 1980s. You'd have been hard-pressed to go to a restaurant that did not have some version of this dish on their menu. I suspect that the new seafood restaurant that Maddie wanted to visit would have had this dish on its menu. This particular recipe is easy to prepare and delicious. Serve it with rice and a vegetable medley on the side.

4 skinless redfish filets, about 8 ounces each, each around 1/2 inch thick. If you can't find redfish, any firm-fleshed fish will work, like pompano or flounder
1 tablespoon paprika
2 1/2 teaspoons kosher salt
1 teaspoon onion powder
1 teaspoon garlic powder
1 teaspoon cayenne pepper
1/2 teaspoon dried thyme
1/2 teaspoon dried oregano
2 sticks unsalted butter, melted, divided
1 package wild rice, cooked according to package instructions
Steamed vegetables, for serving

In a small bowl, combine the spices. Mix well and set aside.

Place a large, heavy nonstick or cast-iron skillet over high heat until very hot.

Pour one stick of the melted butter into a shallow bowl. Dip each filet into the melted butter so that both sides are well coated. Sprinkle the spice mixture evenly on both sides of each piece of fish.

When the skillet is hot, place the prepared filets inside and drizzle half the remaining melted butter over them. Cook uncovered until the underside is blackened, about two minutes. Turn the fish over and pour over the rest of the melted butter. Cook for another two minutes or until done.

Be sure to turn your exhaust fan on high and open a window because this can get a little smoky!

Serve immediately with wild rice and veggies. Serves four.

Pesto Penne

In "The Bride of Tupperman," Season 2, Episode 11, David attempts to find a woman meeting Mr. Tupperman's specifications at the real Beverly Hills Italian restaurant En Brochette. There is still an Italian restaurant at this location, called Il Cielo. This recipe is based on the menu that would have been served at En Brochette and Il Cielo in the 1980s.

  1 16-ounce package penne pasta
  3 cups fresh basil leaves
  2 fresh garlic cloves, smashed and finely chopped
  3 tablespoons pine nuts or walnuts, toasted
  1/2 cup olive oil
  1/2 cup grated Parmesan cheese
  Salt and pepper, to taste
  Extra parmesan cheese, for serving

To make the pesto: Add the basil, garlic, pine nuts (or walnuts), and parmesan to a food processor fitted with the steel blade and pulse until a uniform paste forms. Drizzle in the olive oil. Season to taste with salt and pepper. Cook the pasta according to package instructions and drain, reserving half a cup of the pasta water. Add the drained pasta back to the cooking pot and drizzle in a little olive oil. Immediately add the pesto mixture and stir well to combine. If pasta sauce is too thick, thin with a little reserved pasta water until pasta reaches desired consistency. Serve immediately with extra fresh parmesan over the top. Serves four.

Hobo Packets

David: "Opened a can of beans with my teeth. All right, it was a bag of beans. Found out you're not to eat your beans before you hop the freight train." From "Witness for the Execution," Season 2, Episode 15

In "Witness for the Execution," David is on the run from the law after being framed for the murder of an elderly client. He goes underground, hops a freight train, and hangs out with a group of hobos. This recipe for hobo packets is inspired by this episode. These are equally good over a campfire or in the oven.

1 14-ounce can fire-roasted diced tomatoes, undrained
1 cup chicken broth
1 teaspoon Cajun seasoning
1 cup instant rice, uncooked
1 16-ounce can red beans, drained and rinsed
1 large green bell pepper, seeded and chopped
1 medium onion, diced
2 ribs celery, chopped
1 pound smoked sausage, sliced into half-inch slices
Foil and parchment paper, for hobo packets

In a medium bowl, stir together the tomatoes, chicken broth, and Cajun seasoning. Stir in the rice and let stand at room temperature until most of the liquid is absorbed, about fifteen minutes. Stir in the beans, bell pepper, onions, and celery.

Cut four large pieces of foil and four slightly smaller pieces of parchment paper. Place one piece of parchment paper on top of each piece of foil. Divide the rice mixture evenly across the four packets. Top each with a quarter of the sliced sausage. Fold the long sides together and form a seam, then roll the short sides up to form additional seams. Refrigerate for up to three days.

Cook over a campfire (or grill) on low heat for around thirty minutes, rotating at least once. Or bake at 325 for thirty minutes. Let cool for a couple of minutes and then open up the seams, crush the foil into a bowl shape, and enjoy! Serves four.

Chicken Kiev

In season two's "Every Daughter Is a Virgin," Season 2, Episode 14, Maddie and David meet Maddie's parents, Alex and Virginia Hayes, for dinner at Le Bel Age, inside the Wyndham Bel Age hotel.

This recipe is inspired by the menu at Le Bel Age, a real Los Angeles restaurant that served high-end Russian cuisine. Restaurants serving Russian haute cuisine were extremely popular in the 1980s, as were dishes such as beef stroganoff, chicken Kiev, borscht, and flavored vodkas. New York City's Russian Tea Room, Atlanta's Nikolai's Roof, and Los Angeles's Le Bel Age, as well as other Russian haute cuisine restaurants across America, all catered to this popular 1980s trend. For more information about Le Bel Age, see the "*Moonlighting* Restaurants & Nightclubs: A History" section of this book.

The origins of Chicken Kiev go back as far as the early-nineteenth century, when Russian royalty sent their chefs to France to study classic culinary techniques. A classic chicken Kiev is a bit more complicated than this version, which I have adapted for the home cook, but this recipe is equally delicious.

I like to think Maddie would have enjoyed ordering this dish at Le Bel Age, while David would probably have preferred a beef dish like stroganoff.

For the chicken:
4 boneless, skinless chicken breast halves, about 6 ounces each, lightly pounded to an even thickness
1 stick unsalted butter, softened
2 tablespoons fresh dill, finely chopped
2 tablespoons fresh chives, finely chopped
3 large eggs, beaten
1 cup all-purpose flour
2 cups panko breadcrumbs
2 tablespoons extra-virgin olive oil, plus more for frying
Salt and freshly ground black pepper, to taste

For the side salad:
1 clam case arugula
1 tablespoon freshly squeezed lemon juice (around 2 lemons)
1/4 cup olive oil

Carefully slice a pocket into the side of each chicken breast. Season well with salt and pepper.

In a small bowl, mix the butter, dill, and chives with a wooden spoon until well combined. Spoon a quarter of the butter mixture into each of the chicken breast pockets and pinch closed (or close with toothpicks).

Break the eggs into a shallow bowl or pie plate and whisk well to combine. Add the Panko to another shallow bowl.

Working with one chicken breast at a time, dredge in flour, shaking off the excess, then dip into the egg mixture and then the breadcrumbs. Put the chicken breasts onto a small baking sheet and put in the freezer for five to ten minutes, until set.

Cover the bottom of a large nonstick skillet with olive oil and heat over medium-high until shimmering. Add the chicken breasts and cook for four to five minutes per side or until cooked through.

In a large bowl, whisk the two tablespoons of olive oil and lemon juice. Season with salt and pepper. Add the arugula and toss to combine.

Transfer the chicken to plates and serve with the arugula salad alongside. Serves four.

Baja-Style Fish Tacos

Mexican and Tex-Mex food were extremely popular in the 1980s. This recipe is inspired both by Seaside Fish, David Addison Sr.'s fish market, and David's trip to Mexico, where he would have undoubtedly encountered Baja style fish tacos.

For the fish:
4 pieces (4 ounces each) firm white fish: cod, mahi mahi, or tilapia
3/4 teaspoons chili-lime seasoning
1/2 teaspoon cumin
1/2 teaspoon salt

For the sauce:
1/2 cup sour cream
1 tablespoon freshly squeezed lime juice
3/4 teaspoon chili-lime seasoning
1/4 teaspoon salt
1 tablespoon water, for thinning sauce

For the slaw:
1/4 cup chopped cilantro
1 bag coleslaw mix
1 tablespoon olive oil
1 tablespoon lime juice
1/4 teaspoon salt

Sprinkle the fish with the salt, cumin, and chili-lime seasoning. Combine the ingredients for the sauce in a small bowl. Refrigerate until ready to eat. Toss the slaw ingredients in a medium bowl. Refrigerate until ready to assemble tacos.

Heat a medium skillet over medium-high heat. Add a drizzle of olive oil. Cook the fish for four to five minutes per side, until the fish is charred and cooked through. Break up into large chunks.

Assemble the tacos by placing the slaw on the bottom of each tortilla, topped with the fish and a drizzle of sauce. Serve warm with lime wedges. Serves four.

Petruchio's Ribs

In season three's "Atomic Shakespeare," Season 3, Episode 7, Petruchio marries and woos Katherina, and after a lot of arguing and sparring, they settle into a happy marriage. Katherina prepares a dinner feast for Petruchio, including a large platter of ribs. This recipe has its roots in classic Memphis-style barbecue.

1 slab baby back ribs, around 3 pounds total weight
1/2 cup prepared barbecue sauce

For the spice rub:
2 teaspoons kosher salt
1 teaspoon freshly ground black pepper
1 tablespoon brown sugar
1 teaspoon smoked paprika
1 teaspoon garlic powder
1/2 teaspoon onion powder
1/4 teaspoon cayenne pepper (optional)
1/4 teaspoon salt

Prepare the rack of ribs by peeling the silver skin away from the back of the rib rack.

For the spice rub, stir all the spices together in a small bowl to combine. Sprinkle half of the mixture over the top of the ribs and rub to coat. Flip the ribs over and repeat with the other half of the spice mixture. Wrap the rack of ribs in plastic wrap and refrigerate for at least two hours, or overnight, up to twenty-four hours total.

Preheat the oven to 250 degrees. Line a half-sheet pan with foil. Remove the plastic wrap from the ribs and place them on the prepared pan. Cover with another sheet of foil. Bake for 3 1/2 hours.

Remove the top piece of foil and drain any excess liquid from the pan. Brush the barbecue sauce over the top of the ribs and bake for an additional thirty minutes, until the top is caramelized. Remove from the oven and let rest for fifteen minutes. Slice and serve.

Great side items for this dish are coleslaw, potato salad, collard greens, or macaroni and cheese. Serves four.

Coq Au Vin

In "Sam and Dave," Season 3, Episode 12, David finds out where Maddie and Sam are having dinner—Chez Bray, which is, by the way, NOT a real Los Angeles restaurant (this scene was shot at the Fox Studios Commissary)—and plans to tell Maddie that he loves her. This does not go according to plan, and David ends up joining them for dinner—and a lot of red wine and brandy.

This recipe is a homage both to all the red wine and brandy that David, Maddie, and Sam enjoy at their dinner as well as to high-end restaurant menus of the 1980s, where coq au vin would almost certainly have been featured.

1 whole chicken, cut into pieces (your butcher should be able to do this for you)
2 tablespoons extra-virgin olive oil
1/4 pound bacon, diced
4 whole carrots, peeled and cut into 1-inch pieces
1 medium onion, sliced
2 cloves garlic, finely chopped
2 teaspoons Kosher salt
1 teaspoon freshly ground black pepper

1/4 cup brandy
1 bottle of dry red wine
1 cup chicken broth
5-6 fresh thyme sprigs
1 package frozen baby onions
2 tablespoons unsalted butter, softened
2 tablespoons all-purpose flour

Preheat the oven to 300 degrees. Preheat a large, heavy Dutch oven over medium-high heat. Drizzle in the olive oil and add the bacon. Cook for five to six minutes or until browned. Remove the bacon to a plate and set aside.

Pat the chicken dry with paper towels and season with salt and pepper. Brown the chicken in the bacon fat for five to six minutes, turning to brown evenly. Depending on the size of your Dutch oven, you may need to do this in batches. When the chicken is browned, transfer to the plate with the cooked bacon.

Add the carrots and sliced onions to the pan and cook for ten minutes, stirring occasionally. Add the garlic and cook for another minute. Season with two teaspoons of kosher salt and one teaspoon of freshly ground black pepper.

Add the chicken and bacon back to the pan, along with any juices that have accumulated on the plate. Add the brandy, chicken stock, wine, and thyme sprigs.

Cover the pot with a lid and cook in the preheated oven for forty-five minutes. Remove from the oven and place on the stove.

Stir the flour and butter together and add to the pot. Add the bag of baby onions. Return to the oven and bake for another fifteen minutes.

Suggested side items are mashed potatoes or polenta.

Serves four.

Sam's Rack of Lamb

Maddie is on a late-night stakeout with David in "Maddie's Turn to Cry,", Season 3, Episode 13. Maddie returns home, exhausted, around 2am. She and Sam have this conversation.

> Sam: "Are you in the mood for lamb? It should be ready in about ten minutes. Figured maybe you didn't get a chance to eat."
> Maddie: "You made lamb?"

This is my mother's recipe for rack of lamb, which she served at dinner parties in the 1980s. Rack of lamb crusted with breadcrumbs and mustard was a very chic dinner party and restaurant offering in the 1980s, which explains why both Sam, and later Annie, prepared it. My mom always served this with au gratin potatoes and a green salad.

2 whole racks of lamb, trimmed and frenched (your butcher will do this for you)
1/2 stick unsalted butter, softened
1 1/2 cups panko breadcrumbs
3 cloves garlic, finely chopped
1 tablespoon fresh rosemary, minced
1 tablespoon fresh thyme leaves, minced
3 tablespoons Dijon mustard
1 1/2 teaspoons salt
1 teaspoon freshly ground black pepper

Preheat the oven to 425 degrees. Line a half-sheet pan with foil. In a medium bowl, mix the butter, panko, garlic, herbs, salt, and pepper.

Season both sides of the racks of lamb with salt and pepper. Place the fat side up on the prepared baking sheet. Bake for twenty minutes. Remove from the oven and spread 1 1/2 tablespoons of mustard over the top of each rack of lamb. Spread the panko, butter, and herb mixture evenly across the top of each rack of lamb, pressing gently to make sure it sticks well. Return the lamb to the oven and bake for another twenty to twenty-five minutes or until it reaches your desired doneness.

Remove lamb from the oven and allow it to rest for ten minutes. Cut the lamb into chops and serve hot with the sides of your choice. Serves six to eight.

It's Quite a Clambake

David: "The past few days have been quite a clambake—and I really didn't come dressed for the party."
From "To Heiress Human," Season 3, Episode 15

Northeasterners and West Coasters would call this a clambake. If you're from the Deep South like Cybill and I are, you'd call this a Low Country boil or even Frogmore stew.

I like to prepare my clambake on a half-sheet pan in the oven, instead of boiling. I think it adds more flavor to the dish, plus it's a lot easier than dealing with boiling water!

1 pound baby red potatoes, halved
3 ears of corn, husked and cut into thirds
1 tablespoon extra-virgin olive oil
1 medium yellow onion, sliced
1 pound large shrimp, peeled and deveined, tails on
2 pounds clams, scrubbed
1 pound smoked sausage, sliced into quarter-inch rounds
3 cloves garlic, finely chopped
1 tablespoon Old Bay seasoning
1/2 teaspoon crushed red pepper flakes
1 stick unsalted butter
2 lemons, sliced into wedges
Optional: fresh Italian parsley, chopped, for garnish
Salt and pepper to taste

Preheat the oven to 425 degrees. Add a sheet of parchment paper to a half-sheet pan. Add the corn and potatoes to the prepared sheet pan. Toss with the olive oil and season with salt and pepper. Bake for thirty minutes, until tender. Remove from the oven. Add the clams, shrimp, onions, and sausage to the baking sheet. Melt one stick of butter and stir in the garlic, Old Bay, and red pepper flakes. Drizzle over the seafood and veggies and stir to combine. Add the lemon wedges to the pan. Return the pan to the oven and bake for fifteen minutes or until the clams have opened and the shrimp turn pink. Remove from the oven and sprinkle with the chopped parsley. Serves six.

Hamburgers Cybill Style

There are several *Moonlighting* references to burgers, but probably the most memorable one is from season four's "A Trip to the Moon." Another burger scene is when David and Terri grab burgers after Lamaze class in season four's "Fetal Attraction."

Many of you may remember that Cybill Shepherd was a spokesperson in 1987 for the US Beef Industry Council and Beef Board, whose slogan at the time was "Beef—Real Food for Real People." There is a fun reference to her stint as a spokesperson at the very end of "Maddie Hayes Got Married" as Maddie and David head to the hospital cafeteria to get something to eat.

As Cybill stated in her ads for the beef council, "Sometimes I wonder if people have a primal, instinctive craving for hamburgers. Something hot and juicy and so utterly simple you can eat it with your hands. I mean, I know some people who don't eat burgers. But I'm not sure I trust them." This is Cybill's recipe for burgers, and it is absolutely delicious. Feel free to add cheese and serve at noon for the full *Moonlighting* experience!

1 pound extra-lean ground beef
2 tablespoons minced onion
1 tablespoon coarse grain mustard
1/2 teaspoon dried basil
1/2 teaspoon dried thyme
1/2 teaspoon ground cumin
Cracked black pepper and salt, to taste
4 slices sharp cheddar cheese (optional)
Desired condiments for serving
4 egg twist hamburger buns

Preheat your oven to broil. Mix the ground beef with all of the other ingredients. Divide into four equal portions and form into patties.

Broil the burgers for seven minutes, turning once. Split four egg twist buns. Place a lettuce leaf, burger, tomato slice, and onion slice on each bun. Top with cheese, if desired. Serve with desired condiments.

Serves four.

David's Stakeout Sandwich

In Season 4's "Come Back, Little Shiksa," Season 4, Episode 2, David and Bert are on a stakeout in an attempt to find the mysterious Cinderella-like woman whom their client Donald Chase (guest star John Goodman) asked them to find. David enjoys a turkey sandwich while on their stakeout. This recipe is inspired by his lunch!

2 slices white sandwich bread
4 ounces deli turkey or ham, thinly sliced
2 slices Swiss cheese
1 leaf Boston lettuce
Mayonnaise
Mustard

Spread the mayonnaise and mustard on the bread. Add the turkey, Swiss, and lettuce leaf. Enjoy while following your client on stakeout—or for lunch anytime!

Steak a la Dave

David (message on Maddie's answering machine): "It's Dirty Dave. FYI, yours truly is stopping off at Trader Joe's on the way home, 'cause guess what—I'm making you dinner. Candlelight, vino, and Steak a la Dave. Clear a space on the rug, baby!"
From "A Tale in Two Cities," Season 4, Episode 4

Trader Joe's is a now-nationwide specialty grocery store. At the time of *Moonlighting*, Trader Joe's stores were located only in the Los Angeles area. The first Trader Joe's opened in 1967 in Pasadena, California, and it remains in operation today. In Trader Joe's early days, the stores offered fresh meats provided by butchers who leased space in the stores, along with sandwiches and freshly cut cheeses, all in store. In 1993, Trader Joes expanded to the Pacific Northwest and in 1996 to the East Coast. Today, there are almost six hundred Trader Joe's stores across the United States.

2 filet mignon steaks, around 8 ounces each
1 tablespoon vegetable oil
1 tablespoon Montreal steak seasoning
4 sprigs fresh thyme
2 teaspoons unsalted butter
1 cup whiskey, to deglaze pan

Preheat the oven to 425 degrees. Heat a medium cast-iron skillet over high heat for four to five minutes, until very hot.

Pat the filet mignon steaks dry and rub with the vegetable oil. Sprinkle the steak seasoning evenly around each of the steaks, pressing in to make sure the seasoning sticks well.

Add the seasoned steaks to the hot pan and sear for four minutes per side, around eight minutes total. Be sure to turn on your vent and maybe open a window too!

Turn off the heat and pour in the whiskey. Top each filet with a teaspoon of butter and a couple of sprigs of thyme. Transfer the pan to the oven and cook the steaks for anywhere from eight minutes for rare to twenty minutes for well-done. Serve the steaks with the sides of your choice and glasses of red wine. Serves two.

Irma Addison's Pot Roast

We don't have a lot of the backstory of David's mother, other than his parents are no longer together. And—if you believe the cold opens—she was in an Iron Lung and died after learning that *Moonlighting* didn't win any of the sixteen Emmys it was nominated for in 1986. But we do know in "A Tale in Two Cities," Season 4, Episode 4, Dave swears, "By my Mother's pot roast," to Agnes.

1 4-5 pound chuck roast
1/2 jar sliced pepperoncini peppers
1 packet ranch dressing mix
1 packet onion soup mix
4 tablespoons unsalted butter
2 cups water

Add the chuck roast to a crock pot. Sprinkle the ranch dressing mix and the onion soup mix over the pot roast. Sprinkle the sliced pepperoncini on top. Cut the butter into small pieces and sprinkle over the pot roast. Pour in the water. Cook the pot roast on low for eight hours. Remove the roast from the crock pot and place on a large plate. Remove fat.

Cut up or shred the pot roast and add back to the Crock-Pot. Serve warm with mashed potatoes, rice, or egg noodles and a green vegetable on the side.

Philly Cheesesteaks with Onions

David: "You're a Philly boy too? Why don't you say we walk outta here and get a couple of cheesesteaks with onions?"
From "Cool Hand Dave, Part 2," Season 4, Episode 6

In season four's "Cool Hand Dave, Part 2," David bonds with a fellow prisoner who is also from South Philly. They talk about cheesesteaks, which are something David would have definitely eaten and enjoyed growing up in Philadelphia. This recipe for cheesesteaks uses rare deli roast beef instead of a more traditional wafer-thin sliced ribeye. Feel free to substitute the latter for a more traditional Philly cheesesteak.

2 hoagie or sub rolls
1/2 pound rare deli roast beef, sliced very thin (Boar's Head)
1/2 pound provolone cheese, sliced thin
1 medium yellow onion, thinly sliced
1 green bell pepper, thinly sliced
1 tablespoon extra-virgin olive oil
Salt and pepper, to taste

Heat a large nonstick skillet over medium-high heat. Drizzle in the olive oil and cook the onions and peppers until lightly browned, around six to eight minutes. Season with salt and pepper.

Slide the vegetable mixture to one side of the pan and add the roast beef. Cook until warmed through and no longer pink, around two minutes. Mix together with the veggies, then divide into two portions. Top each portion with half of the provolone and let melt.

Open the rolls and place face down on top of each of the stacks of meat and cheese. Gather the contents into the buns and flip over. Serve immediately. Serves two.

Philly-Style Italian Hoagies

David: "Thought I could interest you in some lunch. Grab a couple of hoagies, sit on the curb, whistle at the babes."
Maddie: "Oh, I'm sorry, I can't. I have plans."
David: "Animal, vegetable, or husband?"
Maddie: "I can't do this today. Let's have lunch tomorrow."
From "Maddie Hayes Got Married," Season 4, Episode 12

David asks Maddie out to lunch, not realizing she has reservations with Walter Bishop at Le St·Germain, one of the nicest restaurants in Los Angeles at the time. I don't know about you, but I'd take hoagies on the curb with David any day over the nicest lunch with Walter!

2 long Italian hoagie rolls
1/4 pound prosciutto
1/4 pound capicola
1/4 pound Genoa salami
1/4 pound hot sopressata salami
1/4 pound provolone, thinly sliced
1/2 cup shredded iceberg lettuce
1 large tomato, thinly sliced
1 small yellow onion, thinly sliced
1/4 cup hot cherry pepper spread
Red wine vinegar, Italian seasoning, salt, and pepper, to taste

Open the rolls lengthwise and scoop out some of the center of the bread. Spread the hot cherry pepper mixture across one side of the bread.

Layer the meats and cheese onto the sandwich, then add the sliced onions, sliced tomatoes, and lettuce. Sprinkle with salt, pepper, and Italian seasoning, then liberally sprinkle on red wine vinegar.

Cut the sandwiches in half and serve. Serves two.

Steamed Vegetable Plate
with Green Goddess Dressing

In "A Womb With a View," Season 5, Episode 1, Maddie is now eating for two and seen enjoying a healthy steamed vegetable plate at lunch. As she eats, we see an enormous floret of broccoli falling past Baby Hayes inside of Maddie's body. This recipe is inspired by her meal.

For the steamed vegetables:
- 1 package broccoli florets
- 1 package cauliflower florets
- 1 cup baby carrots
- 1 cup sugar snap peas
- 1 small package cremini mushrooms, quartered

Bring a cup of water to boil in a saucepan. Add the vegetables to a steamer basket and set over the boiling water. Cover and steam for around eight minutes or until they reach your desired doneness. Serve with green goddess sauce on the side for dipping. Makes four servings.

For the green goddess sauce:
- 1 cup Greek yogurt
- 1 cup fresh Italian parsley
- 1/2 cup sliced green onions
- 1/4 cup fresh dill
- 1/4 cup fresh tarragon
- 2 tablespoons freshly squeezed lemon juice
- 2 tablespoons extra-virgin olive oil
- 1 clove garlic, finely chopped
- 1/4 teaspoon salt
- 1/4 teaspoon freshly ground black pepper

Combine all the ingredients in a food processor or blender and pulse until well combined. Divide into four ramekins or small bowls and serve alongside the steamed vegetables for dipping. Serves four.

David's Meatloaf

David: "Well this has been a hoot, but we've got a meatloaf in the oven back at the trailer park."
From "Between a Yuk and a Hard Place," Season 5, Episode 2

David refers to meatloaf multiple times in "Between a Yuk and a Hard Place." This is a simple, great recipe that I can imagine David making for Maddie.

1 pound ground beef
1 beaten egg
2 slices white sandwich bread, crusts removed, soaked in 1/4 cup milk
1 tablespoon minced dried onion
1/4 cup ketchup
1/4 cup barbecue sauce
1/4 teaspoon salt
1/4 teaspoon pepper
Additional ketchup and barbecue sauce for topping

Preheat the oven to 375. Mix everything together well and press into a loaf pan. Top with a mixture of ketchup and barbecue sauce. Bake for 1 hour or until cooked through. Serves 6.

Bistro Steak Frites

David: "Listen, you don't really want to eat dinner out of a plastic bag, do you?"
Maddie: "I'm not married to the idea."
David: "What are you in the mood for?"
Maddie: "What are you in the mood for?"
David: "Nice little bistro. Couple of steaks. Fortunately, I already made reservations." From "The Color of Maddie," Season 5, Episode 3

Maddie and David discuss the status of their relationship in season five's "The Color of Maddie." David suggests they go out to a nice bistro for steaks, and he has already made a reservation. This is an at-home recipe for bistro style steak frites, featuring New York strip steaks and baked frites.

For the steaks:
2 New York strip steaks, around 10 ounces each
1 tablespoon vegetable oil
1 teaspoon kosher salt
1 teaspoon freshly ground black pepper
4 sprigs fresh thyme
2 teaspoons unsalted butter
1 cup cognac, to deglaze the pan

For the frites:
2 russet potatoes
1 tablespoon extra-virgin olive oil
1 teaspoon kosher salt
1/4 teaspoon freshly ground black pepper
2 tablespoons parmesan cheese
1 tablespoon finely chopped Italian parsley

Preheat the oven to 425 degrees.

For the potatoes:

Add a sheet of parchment paper to a half-sheet pan.

Peel the potatoes and cut into quarter-inch sticks. Toss in a bowl with the olive oil, salt, and pepper. Spread the potatoes onto the baking sheet. Bake, tossing occasionally, until golden brown, about thirty minutes. Remove from the oven, toss with the parmesan and parsley, and serve with the steaks.

For the steaks:

Heat a medium cast-iron skillet over high heat for four to five minutes, until very hot.

Pat the steaks dry and rub with the vegetable oil. Season both sides with salt and pepper.

Add the seasoned steaks to the hot pan and sear for three minutes per side. Be sure to turn on your vent and maybe open a window too!

Turn off the heat and pour in the cognac. Top each steak with a teaspoon of butter and a couple of sprigs of thyme.

Transfer the pan to the oven and cook the steaks for anywhere from eight minutes for rare to twenty minutes for well-done.

Serve the steaks immediately with the frites on the side and glasses of wine. Serves two.

Chicago-Style Hot Dogs

David (to Maddie): "Not too late to go out for some Pink's Hot Dogs. What do you say?" From "Plastic Fantastic Lovers," Season 5, Episode 4

In "Plastic Fantastic Lovers," David offers to take Maddie for a late-night hot dog at Pink's. Since Maddie is a Chicago native, I like to think she would have ordered a Chicago-style hot dog.

Pink's Hot Dogs is one of the most—if not THE most—famous hot dog stands in the country. Pink's is still open today, and you can go visit it in Los Angeles. Pink's is located at 709 North LaBrea Avenue, near Melrose.

A Chicago-style hot dog is an all-beef hot dog in a poppy seed bun and is often described as "dragged through the garden"—topped with diced onions, tomato slices, a dill pickle spear, pickled sport peppers, neon-green Chicago-style relish, yellow mustard, and celery salt. Any Chicago native considers it blasphemous to put ketchup on a hot dog!

1 pound ground beef
4 top-split poppy seed hot dog buns
4 all-beef bun-length hot dogs
1/4 cup Chicago-style relish (this can be difficult to find outside of the Chicago area—you can substitute sweet pickle relish)
1 small yellow onion, finely diced
2 medium tomatoes, halved and thickly sliced lengthwise
4 dill pickle spears
8 sport peppers (these can be difficult to find outside of the Chicago area—you can substitute sliced pepperoncini)
Yellow mustard, to taste
Celery salt, to taste

Grill the hot dogs per package instructions. Toast hot dog buns if desired. Assemble the hot dogs as follows: place a cooked hot dog inside each bun. Top with the yellow mustard, relish, and chopped onion. On one side of each hot dog, add the sliced tomatoes. On the other side, add a pickle spear and two sport peppers (or a few sliced pepperoncini). Sprinkle the hot dogs with celery salt and serve immediately. Serves four

Tortellini "Tre P"

Maddie: "Sounds like he's doing well. Staying at the Bel Air Hotel. Dinner at Adriano's"
From "Brother, Can You Spare a Blonde," Season 2, Episode 1

Adriano's was a real Los Angeles restaurant in the 1980s. For more information about Adriano's, see the "*Moonlighting* Restaurants & Nightclubs: A History" section of this book. This recipe is inspired by a pasta dish on the Adriano's menu in 1985.

   12 ounces refrigerated cheese tortellini
   1/4 cup reserved pasta cooking water
   2 tablespoons butter
   2 minced garlic cloves
   1/4 pound prosciutto, sliced into thin strips
   1 cup heavy cream
   1 pinch nutmeg, freshly grated
   1/4 cup grated parmesan cheese
   1 cup frozen baby peas, thawed
   Salt and pepper, to taste

Cook the tortellini according to package directions. Reserve one-quarter cup pasta cooking water. Drain pasta.

   Melt the butter in a large skillet and add the minced garlic. Cook for one minute or until fragrant. Add the prosciutto and cook for two minutes. Add the heavy cream and bring to a simmer. Add the nutmeg and cook until the cream is thickened and reduced by half. Stir in the parmesan, peas, reserved cooking water, and tortellini and toss to coat. Season with salt and freshly ground black pepper. Serve immediately. Serves two.

– CHAPTER 4 –
DESSERTS

There are many references to desserts and sweet treats in *Moonlighting*. There are cream pies thrown in David's and Maddie's faces during the food fight at the Millennium Biltmore in "The Murder's in the Mail." David, Agnes, and the Wobblies celebrate Maddie's birthday with a cake—and David's rendition of the Beatles' "Birthday"—in "In God We Strongly Suspect." There is an ice cream party in "Cool Hand Dave, Part 2" to help break up a prison riot. Maddie and Walter enjoy Cecil's cocoa on the train from Chicago to Los Angeles in "Tracks of My Tears." Terri offers David a Cookie Monster Swirl dessert after dinner in "Maddie Hayes Got Married." All of these desserts—and more!—add a dose of sweetness and fun to *Moonlighting* and have inspired the recipes in this chapter.

Iced Sugar Cookies

In the opening sequence of "'Twas the Episode Before Christmas," Season 2, Episode 10, we see a festive display in Mary and Joseph's apartment—a Christmas tree and iced sugar cookies cut into star and tree shapes. This is a wonderful recipe for iced sugar cookies that you can enjoy making with your own family.

For the cookies:
3/4 cup sugar
1/3 cup shortening
6 tablespoons butter, softened
1 egg
1 tablespoon milk
1 teaspoon vanilla extract
2 cups all-purpose flour
1 1/2 teaspoon baking powder
1/4 teaspoon salt

For the icing:
1 cup powdered sugar
2 teaspoons milk
2 teaspoons light corn syrup
1/2 teaspoons almond or vanilla extract or a mix
Assorted food coloring

Cream the sugar, shortening, and butter until fluffy. Add the egg, milk, and vanilla. Beat well. Stir together the flour, baking powder, and salt; stir into creamed mixture. Cover and chill for at least three hours.

Working with half of the dough at a time, roll to 1/8 inch thickness on a floured surface. Cut with cookie cutters into desired shapes. Place on a cookie sheet lined with parchment paper. Bake at 375 degrees until set but not browned, about eight minutes.

Note: you can add sprinkles prior to baking or frost and sprinkle after cookies are cool.

For frosting, in a small bowl, stir together the powdered sugar and milk until smooth. Add the corn syrup and extract(s) and mix until the icing is smooth and glossy. Divide into separate bowls and add food coloring to each. Dip one side of each cookie into icing. Add sprinkles if desired and dry on a wire rack.

White Chocolate Banana Cream Pie

"The Murder's In the Mail," Season 1, Episode 6, ends with a huge food fight, with both Maddie and David (and several others) ending up with a cream pie in their face. This recipe is based on a dessert at an iconic 1980s restaurant in Atlanta called the Buckhead Diner (now closed). This pie is just too good to throw at someone—it is best enjoyed sliced and served on a dessert plate with a cup of coffee!

For the pastry cream:
1 cup whole milk
1/2 vanilla bean, split lengthwise
3 large egg yolks
1/3 cup granulated sugar
2 tablespoons cornstarch
1 tablespoon chilled, unsalted butter, cut into pieces
3 ounces high-quality imported white chocolate, finely chopped

For the sweet pastry:
1/2 cup chilled unsalted butter, cut into pieces
1/4 cup plus 1 1/2 teaspoons granulated sugar
2 teaspoons of 1 beaten egg
1 cup plus 2 tablespoons plain all-purpose flour
4 ripe bananas
1 tablespoon freshly squeezed lemon juice
1 1/2 tablespoons banana liqueur

1 1/2 tablespoons white crème de cacao liqueur
2 cups chilled heavy whipping cream, whipped to peaks
Toppings: white chocolate curls and cocoa powder

To make the pastry cream:

Bring the milk and vanilla bean to a boil in a heavy medium saucepan.

In a medium bowl, whisk together the sugar and egg yolks until pale and thick. Whisk in the cornstarch. Whisk one cup of the warm milk into the yolk mixture to temper it. Add that mixture to the remaining milk in the saucepan and whisk until the custard boils and thickens, about thirty seconds. Pour into the bowl and whisk in the butter and white chocolate. Press plastic wrap onto the surface of the pastry cream to prevent a skin from forming. Refrigerate until well chilled. Note: the custard can be prepared up to two days in advance.

To make the sweet pastry:

In a food processor, pulse the butter and sugar together. Add the egg and blend until just combined. Add the flour and pulse to blend, until the mixture resembles coarse meal. Gather the dough into a ball and flatten into a disk. Wrap in plastic and refrigerate at least thirty minutes.

Preheat the oven to 350 degrees. Roll out the pastry on a floured surface to a 13-inch round. Brush off excess flour. Transfer the dough to a 9 1/2-inch pie dish. Crimp the edges. Butter a large foil round and fill with dried beans or pie weights. Set on top of the crimped pie crust. Bake until the crust sides are set, about twelve minutes.

Carefully remove the foil and pie weights. Pierce the dough with a fork. Bake until golden brown, about five minutes. Cool on a rack.

Peel and slice the bananas and toss with lemon juice. Fold into the prepared pastry cream. Fold in the liqueurs. Gently fold half of the whipped cream into the pastry cream.

Spoon filling into pie shell. Top with the remaining whipped cream and chocolate curls. Sift cocoa powdered over the top. Serve immediately (can be prepared thirty minutes ahead).

Crepes Suzette

Casino Restaurant Waiter offers Maddie a menu; she declines.
Maddie: "That won't be necessary. Just bring me the most expensive thing on the menu – two of them!"
Waiter: "And would the lady care for some wine perhaps?"
Maddie: "No, I think I'll have champagne. Dom Perignon '76 if you have it. A magnum will do."
Waiter: "And is the lady expecting a dinner guest?"
Maddie: "No, the lady is expecting to christen a battleship."
From "Money Talks, Maddie Walks," Season 2, Episode 3

When Maddie visits the casino in Buenos Aires—that her ex-accountant opened with her money—she orders the most expensive thing on the menu, which, when it arrives at her table, is a complex flambé dish. I believe this dish is crêpe suzette, a chic, classic dish that was especially popular in the 1980s. Here is a great—and not too complicated—recipe for them.

For the crepes:
1 cup all-purpose flour
1 large egg, beaten
1 1/2 cups milk
2 tablespoons melted and cooled butter
2 teaspoons Grand Marnier or Cointreau
1 pinch salt
Vegetable oil or nonstick cooking spray, for pan

In a medium bowl, combine the flour and the salt. Add the beaten egg and mix well with a wooden spoon.

Whisk in the milk, melted butter, and liqueur. Allow to stand for thirty minutes.

Lightly grease an eight-inch crepe pan or nonstick skillet and heat over medium-high heat. Pour 1/4 cup of the batter into the pan and swirl around to coat. When the crepe has a bubbly surface, carefully flip with a spatula and let it brown on the other side. This will take about thirty seconds per side. Transfer the crepe to a large plate and repeat with remaining batter, re-oiling the pan after every three to four crepes. Use immediately in the recipe or cover with plastic wrap and refrigerate until needed.

For the sauce:
1 cup orange juice
Finely grated zest of one orange
1 1/2 sticks unsalted butter
1/2 cup granulated sugar
1/2 cup Grand Marnier or Cointreau

Add the orange juice, orange zest, butter, and sugar to a medium saucepan. Bring to a boil over medium-high heat. Reduce to medium low and simmer until reduced to a syrup, around ten to fifteen minutes. Remove from heat and set aside.

To assemble the crepes:
Fold the crepes into quarters and arrange in a circular pattern, slightly overlapping, in a nonstick skillet or other shallow flameproof pan. Pour the warm syrup on top and place over low heat until the crepes are warm, about five minutes. Warm the liqueur in the pan that had the orange syrup in it. When the crepes are hot, pour the liqueur on the top and carefully touch a flame to the surface to light it. Serve immediately, spooning the crepes and sauce onto individual dessert plates.

Maddie's Birthday Cake

"In God We Strongly Suspect," Season 2, Episode 13, the Blue Moon employees lure Maddie to David's office with a breadcrumb trail of discarded clothing. When she gets there, they sing the Beatles' "They Say It's Your Birthday" to her and present her with a birthday cake—yellow cake with white frosting. It's a very sweet moment, but Maddie, who doesn't like to have a fuss made over her birthday, isn't thrilled. This recipe for a yellow cake with white frosting is inspired by this scene.

For the yellow cake:
2 1/4 cups all-purpose flour
1 1/2 teaspoons baking powder
1/4 teaspoon baking soda
1/2 teaspoon salt
2 sticks unsalted butter, softened
1 3/4 cups sugar
2 teaspoons vanilla extract
3 large eggs plus 2 large egg yolks, at room temperature
1/2 cup whole milk

1/2 cup sour cream

For the frosting:
2 sticks unsalted butter, softened
3/4 cup powdered sugar
2 teaspoons vanilla extract
2-3 tablespoons whole milk

Tools needed: two round cake pans, offset spatula, mixer

Preheat the oven to 350 degrees and set the oven rack in the lower middle of the oven.

Sift the flour, baking powder, baking soda, and salt together into a large mixing bowl. In a large measuring cup, mix the milk and sour cream together.

With a handheld or stand mixer, cream the butter on medium-high seed for two minutes, until whipped. Add the sugar and beat for another three minutes. Mix in the vanilla. Add the eggs and egg yolks one at a time. Scrape down the sides of the bowl as needed.

Alternate adding the dry ingredients and the milk/sour cream mixture to the butter mixture, mixing well in between additions.

Grease and flour two round cake pans. Line the bottom of each pan with a parchment round. Divide the cake batter evenly between the two pans and shake a bit to settle the batter and minimize air bubbles in the finished cakes.

Bake at 350 for twenty-five to thirty minutes, until the cakes are lightly golden. Test with a toothpick for doneness—it should come out cleanly with a few moist crumbs. Let the cakes rest for ten minutes, and then invert onto wire racks to cool thoroughly before frosting. Remove parchment rounds from the bottom of each cake layer.

For the frosting, cream the butter for around three minutes or until fluffy and lightened in color. Add the powdered sugar half a cup at a time. Mix well after each addition. Mix in the vanilla. Add the milk one tablespoon at a time until the frosting reaches your desired consistency.

When ready to frost, place one cake round on a serving plate. Top with 1/3 of the frosting mixture and spread to the edges using an offset spatula. Top with the second cake layer and the remaining frosting. Frost top and side of cake. Decorate as desired. Serve and enjoy!

Ice Cream Sundaes

In "Cool Hand Dave, Part 2," Season 4, Episode 6, the inmates enjoy an ice cream party as a truce to end the prison riot. They indulge in ice cream with lots of toppings, including chocolate sprinkles, and butterscotch sauce.

In "When Girls Collide," Season 5, Episode 10, David and Annie get ice cream at the famous CC Brown's on Hollywood Boulevard (now closed) and Annie gets the famous ice cream sundae. This hot fudge sauce is based on the real CC Brown's recipe.

Ice Cream Sundaes:

1/2 gallon vanilla ice cream
Hot fudge sauce (recipe below)
Toppings: whipped cream, maraschino cherries, store-bought butterscotch sauce, chocolate sprinkles, anything you like!

Copycat CC Brown's Hot Fudge Sauce

2 cups heavy cream
1/2 stick unsalted butter
1/2 cup light brown sugar
3/4 cup granulated white sugar
1/4 teaspoon salt
2 ounces bittersweet chocolate, cut into small pieces
1 1/4 cups cocoa powder
1 teaspoon vanilla extract

For the sundaes: Scoop ice cream into dishes and serve with the toppings of your choice.

For the sauce: In a medium saucepan over medium-low heat, combine the heavy cream, butter, brown sugar, white sugar, and salt. Bring to a simmer and simmer for one minute. Add the chopped chocolate and whisk to dissolve. Remove from heat and add the cocoa powder. Whisk until smooth.

Return to low heat and simmer the hot fudge sauce until thick and glossy, whisking constantly, around one minute longer. Remove from heat and add the vanilla. Serve warm over ice cream.

Reheat leftover sauce in the microwave or in a saucepan over low heat. Do not boil!

Cecil's Cocoa

Walter: "One of the benefits of frequent rail travel—Cecil's Cocoa. Available to acquaintances of long standing. Hope you like marshmallows!"
From "Tracks of My Tears," Season 4, Episode 10

Maddie meets the infamous Walter Bishop on the train from Chicago to Los Angeles in "Tracks of My Tears." After a few mishaps, they enjoy dinner together on the train. After Maddie's nightmare about David and the train derailment, Walter brings her hot cocoa with marshmallows—a specialty of the train's chef, Cecil.

1/4 cup cocoa powder
2 ounces semisweet chocolate
1/4 cup sugar
1/8 teaspoon salt
4 cups whole or 2 percent milk (don't use skim here)
1 teaspoon vanilla extract
Miniature marshmallows, for serving

Add the cocoa powder, chocolate, sugar, and salt to a medium saucepan. Pour the milk over the top. Place the saucepan over medium heat and whisk until the chocolate has fully melted into the milk. Do not boil!

Remove from the heat and add the vanilla extract. Serve hot in mugs with marshmallows. Serves four.

Cookie Monster Swirl

There is a Midwestern brand of ice cream that offers a Cookie Monster-themed ice cream in the summertime, but Cookie Monster Swirl is a *Moonlighting* invention in "Maddie Hayes Got Married," Season 4, Episode 12. This recipe is an easy layered dessert that allows *Moonlighting* fans to make this simple version of a Cookie Monster Swirl at home all year long, no matter where you live.

> 20 chocolate sandwich cookies, broken into small pieces
> 20 packaged chocolate chip cookies, broken into small pieces
> 1 16-ounce container frozen whipped topping, thawed
> 1 small box instant chocolate pudding
> 2 cups milk
> Blue food coloring
> Toppings: mini chocolate chips and 5 chocolate chip cookies, crumbled

Prepare the chocolate pudding according to package directions. Fold in half of the whipped topping. Sprinkle the crushed chocolate sandwich cookies in the bottom of an eight-by-eight square pan. Top with half of the pudding mixture and spread evenly. Sprinkle the crushed chocolate chip cookies on top of the pudding layer and repeat with the other half of the chocolate pudding mixture. Mix a few drops of blue food coloring into the remaining whipped topping and add to the top of the dish. Garnish with mini chocolate chips. Refrigerate for four hours before serving. When ready to serve, crumble the additional five chocolate chip cookies over the top.

White Chocolate Macadamia Cookies

Maddie: "She's not some nutcase!"
David: "Her middle name is macadamia!"
From "Shirts and Skins," Season 5, Episode 5

Any 1980s-era cookbook would be remiss without the inclusion of macadamia nuts. Macadamias were all the rage in the 1980s, from desserts to ice cream (remember Häagen-Dazs's Macadamia Nut Brittle?) to salads to crusts for main dishes like fish and lamb. This recipe for white chocolate macadamia cookies is one that I think David, with his sweet tooth, would particularly enjoy.

1 1/2 sticks unsalted butter, softened
1/2 cup sugar
1 cup light brown sugar
2 teaspoons vanilla extract
2 eggs
2 1/4 cups all-purpose flour
1 teaspoon baking soda
1/2 teaspoon salt
1 12-ounce package white chocolate chips
8 ounces chopped macadamia nuts

Preheat the oven to 350 degrees. Cream the butter and sugars in a large bowl with a hand mixer until light and fluffy, about three minutes. Add the vanilla and eggs and mix well. Add the flour, baking soda, and salt and mix until blended. Stir in the white chocolate chips and macadamia nuts.

Add a sheet of parchment to a half-sheet pan. Using a cookie scoop or tablespoon, drop the dough onto the prepared cookie sheet. You should be able to fit a dozen cookies on the cookie sheet at a time. Bake for ten to twelve minutes or until the edges and tops are golden brown. Let cool for a few minutes before putting the cookies on a wire rack to cool completely. Repeat with the remaining dough. This recipe makes about two and a half dozen cookies.

Viola Cannoli

Bert to Agnes: "My own grandmother is forcing me to marry someone who eats cannoli for a living." From "In 'N Outlaws," Season 5, Episode 11

This is a simple and easy recipe for cannoli, inspired by the Viola family reunion in season five's "In 'N Outlaws." You can make your own cannoli shells if you want or just get store bought and fill them at home.

- 8 store-bought cannoli shells
- 2 cups ricotta cheese
- 1 cup powdered sugar, plus more for dusting the tops of the cannoli
- 3/4 cup mini chocolate chips
- 2 teaspoons vanilla extract
- 2 teaspoons fresh orange zest

Place the ricotta cheese into a fine mesh strainer. Place in the fridge over a bowl to drain for at least twelve hours (and up to twenty-four hours).

In a large bowl, combine the drained ricotta, powdered sugar, 1/4 cup of the mini chocolate chips, vanilla, and orange zest. Mix well. Using a rubber spatula, scrape the mixture into a pastry bag (or a gallon ziplock bag) fitted with a half-inch star tip.

When ready to serve, pipe the filling into one end of the cannoli shell, filling the shell halfway, then repeat piping into the other end of the shell. Repeat with remaining shells. Place the remaining mini chocolate chips onto a small plate and dip each end of the cannoli into the chocolate chips. Place on a serving platter and dust with powdered sugar using a fine mesh strainer. Serve immediately.

–CHAPTER 5–
BREAKFAST

There are several breakfast-related scenes in *Moonlighting*. Maddie brings breakfast to David to discuss possibly selling Blue Moon in season two's "Atlas Belched." Maddie has breakfast with a client at Hy's Restaurant in Century City in season three's "Big Man on Mulberry Street"—David is running late after a night of too many Vicious Virgins and has forgotten the stakeout photos, and Maddie is furious with him. Sam makes continental breakfast for Maddie at the beginning of season three's "I Am Curious, Maddie." Agnes's mother makes banana waffles for Agnes in season four's "Los Dos Dipestos"—she starts a kitchen fire, and the two end up going out for breakfast instead. This chapter includes recipes inspired by breakfast scenes throughout *Moonlighting*—as well as a special breakfast recipe from Bruce Willis's family that Bruce, aka the Corn Cake King, has made for his family for decades.

David's Sausage and Eggs

David: "You should have my sausage and eggs sometime. Serve it right there on the mattress."
Maddie: "Breakfast on bed. How you."
From "Atlas Belched," Season 2, Episode 9

In season two's "Atlas Belched," Maddie invites David into the office for an early meeting to tell him she is considering selling Blue Moon to Lou LaSalle. In order to soften the blow, Maddie brings a nice breakfast in a picnic basket to share with David, which includes French opera chocolate cake slices, coffee in a thermos, and nice plates and napkins.

David then tells Maddie about his special breakfast of sausage and eggs, which inspired this recipe. I like to think that in the *Moonlighting* Metaverse, Maddie and David enjoyed this breakfast many times during their time together.

6 pork sausage links
4 large eggs
1 teaspoon butter
2 tablespoons shredded sharp cheddar
2 teaspoons milk
Salt and pepper, to taste

Cook sausage links in a medium skillet according to package instructions. Drain on paper towels.

In a medium bowl, whisk together the eggs, milk, salt, and pepper until well combined. Heat a small nonstick skillet over medium-low heat and add the butter, swirling until spread evenly in the pan. Add the egg mixture. Sprinkle in the shredded cheese. Stir the eggs with a silicone spatula or wooden spoon until cooked through, about two minutes.

Divide the eggs and sausage evenly across two plates. Serve in bed, right on the mattress, and enjoy!

Serves two.

Agnes's Favorite Crullers

Agnes: "Bakery? Miss Dipesto at Blue Moon. You know my usual jelly? Make it a cruller!" From "North by North Dipesto," Season 2, Episode 12

After Agnes's exciting evening at the annual Investigators' Ball and the mysteries and chases that follow, she returns to work and orders a cruller instead of her usual jelly donut. Agnes enjoys a cruller and sees them as something special and delicious. This recipe is for an easy oven-baked cruller that you can make at home.

For the crullers:
1 cup water
3 large eggs, at room temperature
1 cup all-purpose flour
6 tablespoons unsalted cold butter, sliced
2 teaspoons sugar
1/4 teaspoon salt

For the glaze:
1 cup powdered sugar
1/2 teaspoon vanilla extract
1/2 teaspoons almond extract
2 tablespoons milk

In a large saucepan, bring the water, butter, sugar, and salt to a boil. Lower heat and add in the flour. Mix well with a wooden spoon. Continue to cook and stir on medium-low heat for about five minutes, being careful not to let the mixture burn. Remove from heat and transfer the dough to a mixing bowl. Use an electric mixer to beat the dough for one to two minutes. Add one egg at a time and mix well.

Preheat the oven to 450 degrees. Place a sheet of parchment paper onto a half-sheet pan. Transfer the dough to a piping bag (or large ziplock bag) fitted with a half-inch star tip. Squeeze the dough into circles onto the prepared cookie sheet, two inches apart. Bake for five minutes. Reduce heat to 350 degrees and bake fifteen minutes more. Turn off the oven and leave in the oven for five more minutes with the door slightly ajar. Remove from the oven and cool. Prepare the glaze by mixing the powdered sugar, vanilla, and milk. Once the crullers have cooled, dip into glaze and let the glaze set. Serve immediately and enjoy! These are best eaten the day they are made or they will get soggy.

# Sam's Continental Breakfast

In the opening shot of season four's "I Am Curious, Maddie," Season 3, Episode 14, we see that Sam has made Maddie a continental breakfast spread, including corn flakes with sliced strawberries, a margarita glass with more sliced strawberries and canned peach slices, a glass of orange juice, a bowl of fruit (apples, bananas, oranges, red grapes), coffee, and creamer, all on Maddie's fanciest white-and-silver bone china. There's also a butter dish with butter. Sam has obviously already eaten—drank half his OJ, and there are toast crumbs on his plate and half an opened banana.

Maddie seems impressed that Sam pulled this breakfast together for her, but let's face it–this breakfast isn't rocket science (no pun intended)—and it doesn't take a particle physics astronaut to make it.

1 small box corn flakes cereal
1 quart 2 percent milk
1 quart fresh-squeezed orange juice
1 pint strawberries, hulled and halved
1 can sliced peaches, drained
Whole wheat bread, for toast
Butter, for toast
Apples, bananas, oranges, and red grapes, for fruit bowl
Coffee and creamer

To recreate Sam's "feast," get out your best china and set your table for two with bowls, salad-sized plates, and coffee cups and saucers, tablecloth, napkins, and flatware.

Fill the two bowls with the corn flakes. Fill two margarita glasses with the sliced strawberries and sliced peaches. Fill a large bowl with the fresh whole pieces of fruit. Toast some whole wheat bread. Make the coffee and pour into a nice silver coffee pot. Put the cream in the creamer.

Serve to the woman you just proposed to and hope she chooses you instead of her smart and sexy private investigator partner!

Serves two.

Mrs. Dipesto's Banana Waffles

In "Los Dos Dipestos," Season 4, Episode 8, Agnes's mother comes to visit and makes breakfast for Agnes. She ends up burning the waffles and starting a kitchen fire, and the two end up going out for brunch instead.

For the waffles:
2 cups buttermilk
1/4 cup vegetable oil
2 large eggs, beaten
1 teaspoon vanilla
2 cups all-purpose flour
3 tablespoons sugar
1 teaspoon baking powder
1/2 teaspoon baking soda
1/2 teaspoon salt
1/2 cup unsalted butter, melted and cooled

For the banana sauce:
1 cup brown sugar
1/2 cup unsalted butter
1/4 cup maple syrup
1 teaspoon cinnamon
1/2 cup heavy cream
1 tablespoon rum OR
2 teaspoons rum extract
2 teaspoons vanilla extract
3 large bananas, thinly sliced
Whipped cream, for serving

To make the waffles: preheat waffle iron and preheat the oven to 250 degrees (for the waffles to sit and stay warm as the others are being cooked). Whisk the buttermilk, eggs, and vanilla together in a large bowl. Combine the dry ingredients in a medium bowl. Add the dry ingredients to the wet ones and stir until just combined. Drizzle in the melted butter and continue to stir until combined. Pour the batter into the waffle iron and cook according to manufacturer's instructions, usually around five minutes. Transfer the cooked waffles to a wire rack in the oven and keep warm. Repeat to cook all of the waffles.

To make the banana sauce: preheat a skillet over medium heat. Add the butter and melt. Stir in the brown sugar, maple syrup, and cinnamon. Bring to a simmer and cook for two to three minutes until smooth and fully combined. Turn down the heat and carefully add the heavy cream. Stir to combine and cook for another three to four minutes, stirring constantly. Add the sliced bananas and cook until the bananas start to soften and caramelize. Remove from heat and stir in the rum (or rum extract) and the vanilla extract. Serve banana sauce over hot waffles. Add whipped cream, if desired. Serves eight.

Shakeratos (with Real Milk)

Maddie: "Being David is a wonderful thing. Being David is like a first kiss, all the time. But it's also scary."
Agnes: "And Walter?"
Maddie: "No, he's not like a first kiss. He's more like that white stuff you put in the coffee. You can always depend on it, hot or cold. But that doesn't mean you stop loving real milk either."
From "Eek! A Spouse!" Season 4, Episode 11

A shakerato is a shaken Italian coffee made with espresso (or very strong coffee), simple syrup, and real milk. This drink is a bit unusual, a little sweet, and much more exciting than your average cup of coffee—just like David! When you shake the espresso with a lot of ice and a little sweetener, it forms a creamy froth on the top.

 6 ounces espresso (or very strong coffee), cooled
 1 tablespoon whole milk
 3 teaspoons simple syrup

Combine the espresso, milk, and simple syrup in a large jar with a lid (or use a cocktail shaker). Fill with ice, cover, and shake vigorously until the mixture is very cold and frothy, about thirty seconds. Strain into two ice-filled glasses and serve. Serves two.

Agnes's Pancakes

"Here's Living With You, Kid," Season 4, Episode 13, includes a dream sequence in which Agnes makes Bert pancakes and orange juice. This recipe is inspired by Agnes's pancakes.

> 2 cups all-purpose flour
> 1/4 cup sugar
> 4 teaspoons baking powder
> 1/4 teaspoon baking soda
> 1/2 teaspoon salt
> 1 large egg, beaten
> 2 teaspoons vanilla extract
> 1/2 stick unsalted butter, melted and cooled
> 2 cups milk
> Maple syrup and butter OR sliced berries and whipped cream

Stir together the dry ingredients in a large bowl. In a separate bowl, whisk together the wet ingredients. Add the wet ingredients to the flour mixture and whisk well to combine. Heat a griddle or large nonstick pan over medium heat and grease with a little butter or vegetable oil. Make the pancakes using a quarter cup measuring cup. You should be able to fit six of them at a time on your griddle. When bubbles appear on the top of your pancakes, flip them over and cook on the other side. Pancakes are done when golden brown. Remove and put on a serving platter. Repeat with remaining batter. Serves four.

Corn Cakes

Bruce Willis is known to make a special breakfast treat for his friends and family: corn cakes, which are pancakes made with corn-muffin mix instead of flour.

Bruce's daughter Tallulah Willis said in a Vogue interview that "My dad loves his oldies. I remember these songs playing in the kitchen as my dad made breakfast. He was the Jiffy Corn Cake King, turning out stacks and stacks of them, pouring cold milk on his while we girls bathed ours in syrup."[1] Bruce's wife, Emma Hemming Willis, said in an interview that "We love cooking breakfast together. Bruce does a different spin on a pancake called corn cakes. Imagine a corn muffin as a pancake—it's delicious. He's pretty famous for them around here."[2]

This is the "official" Jiffy Corn Cake recipe from the side of the Jiffy Corn Muffin box, and I assume it is the same one Bruce uses. These are delicious!

2 packages Jiffy corn muffin mix
2 eggs
4 tablespoons melted butter
1 1/2 cups milk
Maple syrup, butter, and milk for serving

Whisk together the ingredients until large lumps disappear. Preheat a griddle over medium-high heat. Grease the griddle with a little butter or vegetable oil, then pour the batter onto the prepared griddle using a quarter-cup measuring cup of batter for each pancake. You should be able to fit around six pancakes on the griddle at a time.

When pancakes bubble on top and start to brown around the edges, turn them over. Pancakes are done when lightly browned. Remove from the pan and put on a serving platter. Repeat with the remaining batter. Serve warm with maple syrup, butter, and milk. Serves four to six.

---

1   Tallulah Willis, "Tallulah Willis on Grief, Healing, and the Road Ahead," *Vogue*, June 2, 2023.

2   Terry Zeller, "Meet Bruce Willis' Wife, Emma Hemming Willis," *Hollywood Life*, February 16, 2023.

–CHAPTER 6–
"MOONLIGHTING" RESTAURANTS & NIGHTCLUBS—A HISTORY

While much of the *Moonlighting* series was filmed at Fox Studios, many scenes were shot on location in and around Los Angeles. Several scenes were filmed in real-life Los Angeles restaurants, nightclubs, and hotels. This chapter is devoted to the history of the restaurants and nightclubs featured in *Moonlighting*—some of which are still open and can be visited today! Recipes inspired by these real-life restaurants are incorporated throughout this cookbook. All menus are from the Los Angeles Public Library's digital archives.

La Serre

12969 Ventura Boulevard
Studio City, Los Angeles
(Closed in 1991)

La Serre was a high-end Los Angeles restaurant in the San Fernando Valley that opened in 1974.[1] It is where Glenn Gordon Caron and Jay Daniel first met with Cybill Shepherd in 1984 to discuss *Moonlighting*.

The restaurant had a number of small dining rooms decorated with white trellises, plants, rustic brick floors, French provincial chairs, and sunny yellow tablecloths. In its review of La Serre, the *Los Angeles Times* noted that it was "cool and inviting with its white lattices and groomed greenery. La Serre looks like an opulent garden in too small a space. There are potted flowers, cut flowers, ferns, and lots of barely restrained ivy crouched in pots on the wall. The space is divided into several small

---

1   Mimi Sheraton, "Los Angeles Comes of Age in French Cuisine," *New York Times*, November 7, 1979.

rooms. The food is consistently satisfying."[2]

La Serre served stylish (and expensive) French cuisine and was known for both excellent service and delicious food. It was a favorite for power lunches because of the privacy of the rooms and attracted both Hollywood elite and upscale business people. It was an upscale Los Angeles favorite until it closed its doors in 1991.[3]

Interior Photos of La Serre:

---

[2] Michael Hutchings, "La Serre—My Early Career," Coastal Cooking with Chef Michael Hutchings, February 3, 2018, blog.michaelscateringsb.com.

[3] John Johnson, "Valley Loses Prestigious Restaurant: La Serre," *Los Angeles Times*, November 13, 1991.

La Serre Menu, 1980s:

Hong Kong Café

425 Gin Ling Way, Chinatown, Los Angeles
From the *Moonlighting* Opening Credits
(closed; now Stay)

The neon-lit pagoda of Hong Kong Café in Los Angeles's Chinatown was used in the show's opening credits for the first three seasons.

The restaurant's structure was built in Chinatown's Central Plaza in 1939. Restaurant by day and club by night, The Hong Kong Café, located at 425 Gin Ling Way, across the street from rival restaurant Madame Wong's, was a Los Angeles venue that was an integral part of the punk and New Wave music scene during the late 1970s and early 1980s, playing host to some of the hottest artists of the time, including Dead Kennedys, the Alley Cats, and Black Flag.

The Hong Kong Café closed its doors in 1995. After several years as a gift shop, it is currently home to Stay, a cocktail lounge devoted to serving all nonalcoholic drinks.[6]

The Hong Kong Café also appears in the 1974 movie *Chinatown*.

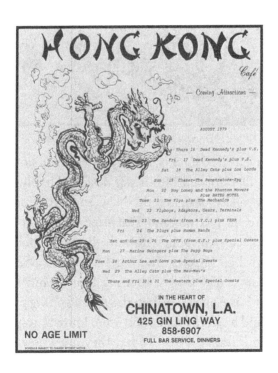

---

6   Bill Addison, "A Gorgeous New Drinking Destination for Dry January (and Beyond)," *Los Angeles Times*, January 13, 2024.

The Starline Room (Bar) and Top of Five (Restaurant)

(now BonaVista Lounge and LA Prime Steak House)
404 South Figueroa Street, Los Angeles
Top of the Westin Bonaventure Hotel
From the Pilot, Season 1, Episode 1

David: "Oh wow! Lobster! My favorite!"

The Westin Bonaventure Hotel is a thirty-three-story hotel that opened in Los Angeles in December 1976. It was designed by the architect John G Portman Jr., who also designed the New York Marriott Marquis, the Renaissance Center in Detroit, and Peachtree Center in Atlanta. It was one of the first projects to be built within the Bunker Hill Redevelopment Area of downtown Los Angeles. The hotel features 1,358 rooms as well as several restaurants, including a rotating lounge and restaurant with sweeping views of Los Angeles.[6] When the *Moonlighting* pilot was filmed, the rotating bar and adjacent restaurant were known, respectively, as the Starline Room and Top of Five.[7] Today, they are known as BonaVista Lounge and LA Prime—and you can still order a lobster dinner there!

---

6   Helen Rumbelow, "Up Here, One Drink and You Start Spinning," *Los Angeles Times*, September 28, 1995.

7   Glen Gordon Caron, "Pilot," *Moonlighting* DVD Commentary, May 31, 2005.

The Westin Bonaventure hotel, its rotating lounge and restaurant, and its elevators figure pivotally in the pilot of *Moonlighting*. Maddie is on a date here with an obnoxious plastic surgeon when David crashes their date to try to convince Maddie not to close the detective agency. While he's there, Maddie's date has to leave for a medical "emergency," and Maddie and David find themselves embroiled in a mysterious plot involving a wristwatch.

The Westin Bonaventure Hotel has been featured in a number of other television shows and films as well, including *True Lies, In the Line of Fire, Forget Paris, Logan's Run, Xanadu, Time After Time, Alias,* and *It's a Living*.[8]

LA Prime as it looks in 2024
Courtesy Westin Bonaventure Hotel Website

---

8   Angeline Woo, "I Sent on a Date . . . with L.A. Here's My Love Letter, Through Photos," *Los Angeles Times*, February 21, 2023.

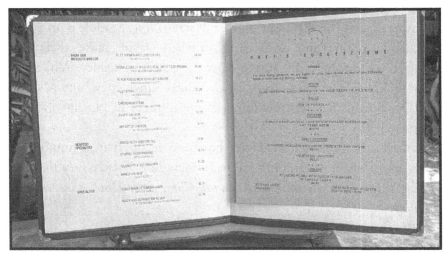

1980s Menu, Top of Five, Westin Bonaventure Hotel

1980s Drink Coasters [below]
from the Starline Room, Westin Bonaventure Hotel

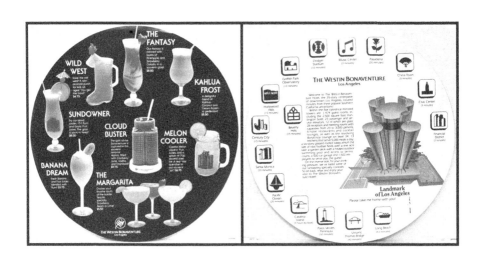

Adriano's Ristorante

2930 Beverly Glen Circle, Los Angeles
(now closed)
From "Brother, Can You Spare a Blonde?" Season 2, Episode 1

Maddie: "Davey and Richie. I never even knew you had a brother!"
David: "I never thought of him as a brother. I always thought of him as Mom and Dad's science project."
Maddie: "How long has it been since you've seen him?"
David (looks at his watch): "This is the eighties?"
Maddie: "Sounds like he's doing well. Staying at the Bel Air Hotel. Dinner at Adriano's."

Moonlighting fans will recognize Adriano's Ristorante as the place where David and Maddie meet David's brother Richie for dinner in the season two premiere, "Brother, Can You Spare a Blonde?" Richie gets an unexpected call, and they leave the restaurant abruptly and go dancing instead.

Adriano's was a popular gathering spot for the entertainment industry for more than two decades. Before closing its doors in 1998, Adriano's was located on Beverly Glen Circle just south of Mulholland Drive, just below the crest of Beverly Glen. It opened in January 1979 with a party hosted by Grease producer Alan Carr.[9]

Adriano's was known for its intimate setting and wonderful Italian cuisine and attracted Hollywood stars, agents, and studio and network executives. It was one of Los Angeles's most beloved Italian restaurants.[10]

---

9   Max Jacobson, "Breezy Summer Fare," *Los Angeles Times*, July 16, 1998.
10 A Times Staff Writer, "A Rebora, 63, Ran Popular Restaurant," *Los Angeles Times*, January 3, 2003.

Menu, Adriano's Ristorante

En Brochette

9018 Burton Way, Beverly Hills
(Closed—now Il Cielo)
From "Bride of Tupperman," Season 2, Episode 11

En Brochette, a Beverly Hills Italian restaurant located inside a tiny bungalow, was featured in "The Bride of Tupperman" as David wanders the city looking for the perfect match for Mr. Tupperman. He finds several beautiful women sitting outside drinking cocktails—all of whom throw their drinks in his face when he approaches them with Mr. Tupperman's offer.

En Brochette opened in Beverly Hills in the 1970s and was sold in 1986 to a man named Pasquale Vericella, who opened his own restaurant in this location called Il Cielo, which means "the sky" in Italian.

The *Los Angeles Times* said, "This is surely one of the loveliest restaurants in Los Angeles. The small dining rooms are light and charmingly rustic, and there's not a nicer outdoor eating area in town. Both the menu and the service are appealing and very Italian." Il Cielo has been voted the most romantic restaurant in Los Angeles several times and named one of the top places in the country to hold a wedding reception by the *New York Times*.[11]

---

11   Jane Greenstein, "Isn't It Romantic?" *Los Angeles Times*, September 20, 1987.

Il Cielo has been the filming location for several other series and movies as well, including *Entourage*, *The Hills*, *Legally Blonde*, and *Spanglish*. It is popular with celebrities. Brad Pitt took Gwyneth Paltrow here on their first date, and Lesley Ann Warren was married here.[12]

Il Cielo is still open today, and you can visit for a nice brunch, lunch, or dinner.

Le Bel Age Restaurant
1020 North San Vicente, West Hollywood
Inside the Wyndham Bel Age Hotel
(Hotel and restaurant both now closed—the hotel is now the London West Hollywood, and the restaurant is now the Boxwood)
From "Every Daughter's Father Is a Virgin," Season 2, Episode 14

David: "Yow, look at this place. I bet even the cockroaches wear tuxedos."

In "Every Daughter's Father Is a Virgin," Maddie and David meet Maddie's parents, Alexander and Virginia Hayes, for dinner at Le Bel Age. Maddie plans to tell her mother about her father's infidelity but decides not to. The four of them end up ordering champagne and enjoying a nice dinner before David walks Virginia back to her room while Maddie and her father go for a walk—and she pummels him with her purse while confronting him about his affair.

Le Bel Age opened inside Wyndham Bel Age in April 1985. The *Los Angeles Times* had this to say about it: "Le Bel Age is so luxurious it makes

---

12   Lindsay Blake, "Los Angeles Filming Locations: Il Cielo," I Am Not A Stalker, June 18, 2009, iamnotastalker.com/tag/il-cielo/.

you feel wicked. In this rosy little world, people look more gracious, move more slowly, and eat with serious sensuality. Soft music envelops you as you sink into the overstuffed pink banquettes; the Franco-Russian food is rich, the service obsequious. Feel guilty if you must, but order the five-course dinner. This is a restaurant for unbridled hedonism." Le Bel Age was also known for its extensive collection of original art pieces.[13]

The restaurant rebranded itself as Diaghilev in 1991 and closed its doors for good in 2008 when the hotel was remodeled and transformed into the London West Hollywood. It later became Gordon Ramsey at the London West Hollywood and, later still, the Boxwood.[14]

The films *Prizzi's Honor* and *St. Elmo's Fire* also feature scenes filmed in Le Bel Age and Wyndham Bel Age, as did the television series *Beverly Hills 90210*.

Menu, Le Bel Age

---

13 Steven Smith, "A Little Romance," *Los Angeles Times*, May 25, 1986.

14 Charles Perry, "Nouvelle Russe: Diaghilev Offers Caviar, Vodkas, Blinis, Borscht, Great Service—and Prices as High as the Urals," *Los Angeles Times*, April 28, 1991.

Hy's Restaurant

10131 Constellation Blvd, Century City
(now closed)
From "Big Man on Mulberry Street," Season 3, Episode 6

Hy's Restaurant is featured in the opening scenes of "Big Man on Mulberry Street" as the location where Maddie meets a client for breakfast and David is running late.[15] In the opening sequence, you can see restaurant staff preparing and serving breakfast, and the camera pans across several tables where diners are having conversations before focusing in on Maddie and her client. David arrives after a time, hung over, disheveled, and without the important photos that the client needs.

Hy's featured banquet rooms, evening jazz and dancing, and "affordable elegance." It was located around the corner from the Shubert Theatre and across the street from the Century Plaza Hotel and ABC Entertainment Center. Ironically, the restaurant did not serve breakfast but was known for its charcoal-broiled steaks, lamb, and seafood.[16]

Hy's opened in 1985. It was known as the Princess Restaurant until purchased by Rod Gardiner. The *Los Angeles Times*'s food critic Ruth Reichl wrote when it opened that "Los Angeles' newest steak house, Hy's in Century City, doesn't look like one. It is far too pretty. It is far too quiet too. You can actually have a civilized conversation while you watch your steak being grilled on that ridiculously rococo grill ensconced in its own little glass room. This is a place that makes you feel pampered. If you order a salad, they roll a cart over and toss it at the table. I think it's the tastiest steak you can get in Los Angeles. It is also one of the

---

15   Jay Daniel, "Big Man on Mulberry Street," *Moonlighting* DVD Commentary, May 31, 2005.
16   Ruth Reichl, "Steak Houses: The Fat & the Lean," *Los Angeles Times*, December 22, 1985.

most reasonable."[17] The Century City location is sadly now closed, but as of this writing, Hy's has steakhouses in Canada in Toronto, Winnipeg, Calgary, Vancouver, and Whistler.

---

17   Kathie Jenkins, "Dining Out in Century City," *Los Angeles Times*, June 11, 1989.

Metropolis Nightclub

650 North La Cienega Boulevard, Los Angeles
(Closed in the 1990s—now Catch Steak)
From "Blonde on Blonde," Season 3, Episode 11

> Bert: "Metropolis! This is the hottest place in town. I've heard about this place. You can't walk in without getting hit on. A real face place. I'm telling you, if you're ever in the mood to meet someone just for the night, this is the place to go."
> David: "Herbert, remember when you asked if you were talking too much?" (rolls his eyes)

In "Blonde on Blonde," Maddie decides to meet a guy at a bar for a one-night stand. She chooses to go to Metropolis, where she orders a boilermaker and gets hit on by multiple guys. David and Bert follow her.

Metropolis served Mediterranean cuisine interpreted by Japanese chefs.[18] In her 1986 review in the *Los Angeles Times*, restaurant critic Rose Dosti said, "I like Metropolis, first of all because of the ambiance. I like all that professional, architectural stuff going on in a restaurant. I like the order and cerebral nature of it. I like the balance and harmony that good interior design brings. This place is a showplace of modern design with materials—woods, concrete, lacquer—that make you think you are in Tokyo. Personally, I appreciate the food, too, because, for

---

18 Jane Greenstein, "Crossing Cultures," *Los Angeles Times*, February 8, 1987.

one thing, it is of excellent quality and very fresh. I also appreciate the chef's interpretation of Mediterranean cooking, just as I would a good American chef's interpretation of Japanese food."[19]

Metropolis Menu, 1980s

Matchbook from Metropolis Bar & Restaurant, Los Angeles

---

19   Rose Dosti, "Mediterranean Cuisine, as Interpreted by Japanese Chefs in LA's Metropolis," *Los Angeles Times*, December 11, 1986.

Earl Carroll Theatre
6230 Sunset Boulevard, Hollywood, California
From "The Dream Sequence Always Rings Twice,"
Season 2, Episode 4

The Earl Carroll Theatre was a glamorous art deco dinner theater and supper club that opened in 1938 in Hollywood on Sunset Boulevard, attracting celebrities, travelers, and locals with its beautiful architecture and luxurious interior spaces. It was known for reinventing dinner theater and the Hollywood nightclub scene with its grand productions and attention to detail. It was, for a time, known as the Aquarius Theatre and was the home of the musical production of *Hair* in Los Angeles. Later, from 1997-2017, it served as Nickelodeon's production studios.

The Earl Carroll Theatre is one of the last remaining examples of modern entertainment venues constructed at the height of Hollywood's Golden Age and has won landmark status as a Historic Cultural Monument, protecting it from demolition.

It was the perfect choice for the Flamingo Cove nightclub in season two's "The Dream Sequence Always Rings Twice." The movies *Harum Scarum*, *Imitation of Life*, and *Kiss Me, Stupid* were filmed here. The theater played host to the Emmy Awards in 1955 and 1961 and the

American Music Awards in 1974.[20]

Menus from The Earl Carroll Theatre, 1940s
Courtesy of The Culinary Institute of America's Online Archive

---

20   The Los Angeles Conservatory, "The Earl Carroll Theatre", December 11, 2024, laconservancy.org.

L'Orangerie
903 North La Cienega Boulevard, Los Angeles
(closed in 2006—now Nobu)

David: "Miss Dipesto, make a lunch date for Ms Hayes and myself. Say 12:30. Say L'Orangerie."
Agnes: "Say no more!"

In "A Tale in Two Cities," Season 4, Episode 4, Agnes and David get to the office and think—incorrectly – that Maddie has returned from Chicago. David asks Agnes to make a lunch date at this restaurant, which, unfortunately, doesn't happen.

L'Orangerie was considered Los Angeles's best—and—most expensive—French restaurant. It opened in 1979 and closed after its New Year's Eve service on December 31, 2006.[21]

The *Los Angeles Times* wrote that L'Orangerie was "one of the most beautiful restaurants anywhere—crossing the threshold is like walking right into the eighteenth century. The light is so golden you can barely believe it's electric. Music, flowers, perfume—it's easy to imagine the waiters doing a minuet. Celebrity regulars included Ronald and Nancy Reagan, and Kirk and Anne Douglas. For several years, L'Orangerie played host to the pre-Oscars dinner.[22]

Today, the former L'Orangerie space houses the famous Japanese restaurant Nobu. Wouldn't we *Moonlighting* fans have loved to have seen David and Maddie dine here?

---

21 Lesley Balla, "L'Orangerie Through the Years," Eater Los Angeles, December 27, 2006, la.eater.com.

22 S. Irene Virbila, "We'll Always Have Paris—at L'Orangerie," *Los Angeles Times*, June 4, 2003.

Le St. Germain
5955 Melrose Avenue, Los Angeles

Agnes: "Ms. Hayes had me make lunch reservations. Twelve o'clock. St. Germain. Table for two."

In "Maddie Hayes Got Married," Season 4, Episode 12, Maddie has Agnes make lunch reservations for her and her new husband, Walter Bishop, at Le St. Germain. Le St. Germain was opened at 5955 Melrose Avenue in Los Angeles in 1970 by a Belgian expat, Paul Bruggemans. It was one of the city's top restaurants, serving an upscale continental menu. It closed its doors in 1988.[23]

The *Los Angeles Times*'s food critic Ruth Reichl said that "Le St. Germain wraps itself around you as you walk in the door, enclosing you in the sort of luxurious intimacy you just don't find much anymore. As you walk through these dimly lit, rose-colored rooms and sink into your seat, the outside world disappears. This is an old-fashioned restaurant that caters to your every whim doing its best to convince you that you are being served in a private home. You never even see a menu. The maître d' simply comes over and tells you about [what is being served that day]."[24]

---

23   Ruth Reichl, "Adieu to St. Germain," *Los Angeles Times*, November 4, 1988.
24   Colman Andrews, "Time for Le St. Germain Rumors Again," *Los Angeles Times*, June 19, 1988.

Callender's Grill
5773 Wilshire Blvd Los Angeles
(now closed)

In "Fetal Attraction," Season 4, Episode 9, David and Terri meet at Callender's Grill for burgers after Lamaze class. And in "And The Flesh Was Made Word," Season 4, Episode 14, Maddie and David have breakfast al fresco while following a client.

Callender's Grill was Marie Callender's flagship boutique restaurant. It opened in 1978 in Los Angeles at Museum Square and remained in operation for more than forty years. Callender's Grill was a deviation from the traditional Marie Callender's restaurants with a more upscale decor. It was known for dishes such as burgers and Philly melts, and some higher-end menu items, as well as an endless display of pies. It also featured a full cocktail menu and an exclusive California wine selection. The famous Callender's Grill Cheeseburger featured lettuce, tomatoes, pickles, Thousand Island dressing, and aged American cheese.[25]

---

25 Mona Holmes, "After A 40 Year Run, Mid-Wilshire's Marie Callender's Closes This Sunday," Eater Los Angeles, July 10, 2018, la.eater.com.

Pink's Hot Dogs
709 North La Brea Avenue, Los Angeles
(still open today)

David (to Maddie): "Not too late to go out for some Pink's Hot Dogs. What do you say?"

In "Plastic Fantastic Lovers," Season 5, Episode 4, David offers to take Maddie for a late-night hot dog at Pink's.

Pink's Hot Dogs was founded in 1939 by Paul and Betty Pink as a pushcart near the corner of La Brea Avenue and Melrose Place, in the Fairfax District of Los Angeles, just west of Hollywood. They sold custom-made natural casing hot dogs with chili, mustard, and onions. Their famous chili dogs were so popular that the family was able to open the current brick-and-mortar building in 1946, and it has been open for business ever since. They have a number of menu items named after celebrities (sadly there are no Bruce Willis or Cybill Shepherd dogs!).

Pink's is open from 9:30 a.m. to midnight every day—and until 2:00 a.m. on Friday and Saturday nights.

Chez Jay
1657 Ocean Avenue, Santa Monica

Agnes (to Bert): "Don't get to Chez Jay later than 7:00 p.m. or you'll ruin the surprise." From "A Womb with a View," Season 5, Episode 1

Chez Jay is the site of the wonderful (until tragedy struck) baby shower that Blue Moon throws for Maddie.

Jay Fiondella opened Chez Jay in 1959. It is a place known for its famous clientele, friendly atmosphere, privacy, and great food. The interior features checkered tablecloths and framed movie posters.[26]

Chez Jay is famous for its wonderful steaks and seafood as well as its free peanuts. One of those peanuts went to the moon with Alan Shepard and became, as Jay Fiondella recalled, the first "astro nut," and that nut still resides in the restaurant's safe.[27] The moon and astronaut references are not lost on us *Moonlighting* fans!

Over the years, Chez Jay has become a celebrity hangout, and its regular patrons have included Fred Astaire, Judy Garland, Jim Morrison, Frank Sinatra, Sammy Davis, Dean Martin, Lee Marvin, Peter Sellers, Richard Burton, the Beach Boys, Warren Beatty, and Marilyn Monroe. Blake Andrews and Julie Andrews had their first date at Chez Jay. It has a curtained-off booth in the back, Table #10, for special celebrity guests.

---

26 Margaret Wappler, "Old Hollywood Lingers at Chez Jay," *Los Angeles Times*, February 24, 2012.
27 Chez Jay, "Chez Jay—About Us," Chez Jay Restaurant Website, October 10, 2024, chezjays.com.

Photos are not allowed—a house rule since the days of Marilyn Monroe and JFK's secret rendezvous in the 1960s.[28]

Located half of a block south of the Santa Monica Pier, next to Tongva Park, it was declared a Santa Monica Historic Landmark in 2012.

Chez Jay is still open today, and you can go visit for a meal!

---

28 Martha Groves, "Santa Monica's Chez Jay Eatery Designated a Local Landmark," *Los Angeles Times*, October 10, 2012.

Spago
176 North Canon Drive, Beverly Hills
(still open today)

Annie (to Maddie): "First I thought we could catch Sean Penn beating on the paparazzi at Spago."
From "When Girls Collide," Season 5, Episode 10

Spago is celebrity chef Wolfgang Puck's flagship restaurant, known for serving California cuisine. The restaurant opened on January 16, 1982, on the Sunset Strip in West Hollywood. The original Spago Hollywood remained open until 2001. Today, there is a Spago at the Bellagio in Las Vegas and on Canon Drive in Beverly Hills as well as in Maui, Istanbul, and Singapore City. Spago has been awarded two Michelin stars, and in 2013 Zagat named Spago the most iconic restaurant in Los Angeles.[29]

Spago was an instant sensation. The Hollywood Reporter declared it "the newest celebrity in town" and "the latest hottest hangout."[30] Its open-kitchen concept was unique[31]—today you will be hard pressed

---

29 Betty Hallock, "Michelin Ratings Have LA Chefs Starry-Eyed," *Los Angeles Times*, November 10, 2007.

30 Seth Abramovitch and Evan Nicole Brown, "Hollywood Flashback: 40 Years Ago, Spago Changed Restaurants Forever," *The Hollywood Reporter*, January 13, 2022.

31 Garrett Snyder, "How Spago Changed Everything," Resy Website, September 16, 2022, blog.

to find a restaurant without an open kitchen! Paparazzi flocked to the parking lot of Spago to snap photos of such A-List regulars as Johnny Carson, Michael Caine, Dolly Parton, Burt Reynolds, Sylvester Stallone, Barbra Streisand, George Lucas, and Steven Spielberg.[32]

---

32 Crystal Coser, "The Spago Timeline: How Wolfgang's Fine Dining Favorite Has Changed Over Three Decades," Eater Los Angeles Website, January 30, 2015, la.eater.com.

CC Brown's Ice Cream

7007 Hollywood Boulevard, Los Angeles
(now closed)
From "When Girls Collide," Season 5, Episode 10

After taking Maddie and her cousin Annie dancing, David takes both of them home, and Maddie goes to bed. David and Annie stay up late talking, then head out for a walk along Hollywood Boulevard. They get ice cream from CC Brown's—David gets a milkshake (we can only imagine that it's his favorite, chocolate), and Annie gets one of its famous hot fudge sundaes. A waiter/mime steals the cherry off of the top of Annie's sundae.

Clarence Clifton Brown opened CC Brown's Ice Cream in downtown Los Angeles in 1906, and his son Cliff moved the family business to 7007 Hollywood Boulevard, just down the street from Grauman's Chinese Theater. It is famous for being the birthplace of the hot fudge sundae.[33]

CC Brown's was a popular celebrity hangout. Regulars over the years included Mary Pickford, Joan Crawford, Bob Hope, and Marlon

---

33 William Campbell, "CC Brown's Ice Cream Parlor Closes," *Los Angeles Times*, June 14, 1996.

Brando.³⁴ It was also a popular spot for a sweet treat after a night out at the movies. CC Brown's closed in 1996.³⁵

---

34 Mark Evanier, "CC Brown's," Old Los Angeles Restaurants Website, February 14, 2012, oldlarestaurants.com.

35 *New York Times* Staff Writer, "Ice Cream Parlor of Stars Is Closing," *New York Times*, June 9, 1996.

Market Street
72 Market Street, Venice, California

Maddie (to Agnes): "I'm taking Annie shopping and to lunch. Would you make a reservation at Market Street, please?"
From "When Girls Collide," Season 5, Episode 10

Maddie and her cousin Annie have lunch at Market Street and enjoy margaritas and flirting with a handsome businessman.

Market Street was a popular Venice Beach restaurant that opened in August 1984. It was a casual, fine-dining eatery founded by the actor and director Tony Bill and the actor Dudley Moore and served traditional American comfort food.

Market Street was a celebrity hot spot and received nationwide attention for its food as well as an in-house radio talk show and lecture series. A cookbook detailing its recipes, which included portraits of its celebrity patrons and their involvement in the restaurant, was published in 1999. Market Street closed in November 2000.[36]

---

36   *Los Angeles Times*: "The '80s: From Nouvelle to Anything Goes," December 24, 1989.

CAROLYN MERRITT GANDY

STARTERS FROM THE OYSTER BAR

OYSTERS ON THE HALF SHELL
BROILED OYSTERS with pesto and garlic ... 12.
CLAMS ON THE HALF SHELL ... 8.
COLD MARINATED MUSSELS with saffron and tomato ... 9.
JUMBO SHRIMP ... 12.
CEVICHE OF BAY SCALLOPS AND PACIFIC RED SNAPPER ... 8.
CALAMARI AND ARTICHOKES with olives, capers, garlic and extra virgin olive oil ... 9.
CHILLED CRAYFISH with spicy garlic mayonnaise ... 10.
COMBINATION PLATTER (all of the above) for up to 4 people ... 40.
($10.00 extra per additional person)

STARTERS FROM THE KITCHEN

SMALL BOWL OF KICK ASS CHILI with cornbread and condiments ... 7.
MIXED FIELD GREENS with extra virgin olive oil and balsamic vinegar ... 7.
CAESAR SALAD with or without garlic ... 7.
HEARTS OF ROMAINE with creamy Iowa Maytag blue cheese dressing ... 7.
ITALIAN BUFFALO MOZZARELLA AND GRILLED RADICCHIO with extra virgin olive oil ... 9.
A SERVICE OF SMOKED SCOTTISH SALMON with walnut wheat toast ... 12.
A SALAD OF SMOKED SALMON, BELGIAN ENDIVE AND ARUGULA ... 10.
GRILLED SHRIMP SALAD with dill oil and Japanese vinaigrette ... 12.
CHICKEN SALAD with baby lettuces, roasted peppers, sundried tomatoes, pine nuts
                and goat cheese ... 10.
CRISPY DUCK AND FRISEE SALAD with fennel, pearl onions, shiitake & tree mushrooms ... 10.
STEAMED CLAMS with ginger, garlic and cilantro ... 10.
CRABCAKES AND CAVIAR: GOLDEN ... 12.
                        SEVRUGA ... 24.

PIANO NIGHTLY

Wine and desserts brought into the restaurant are subject to additional charges.   For further
information, please see respective menu or consult the host or hostess.

MAIN DISHES

STEAMED VEGETABLES AND BAKED POTATO
    with Japanese vinaigrette OR warm olive oil, garlic and lemon juice ... 12.
SAUTEED CAJUN STYLE CATFISH with tartar sauce, cole slaw and fries ... 16.
GRILLED FREE-RANGE CHICKEN with garlic, oregano and tomatillo salsa ... 18.
    (white meat only - $2.00 additional)
MIXED GRILL ON A STICK, served with wild rice ... 18.
GRILLED LOUISIANA SAUSAGES with spinach and mashed potatoes ... 14.
GRILLED VEAL CHOP with warm mushroom vinaigrette, wild mushrooms,
    baby artichokes and extra virgin olive oil ... 26.
ROASTED RACK OF LAMB with gratin potatoes ... 26.
GRILLED PRIME FILET MIGNON with hot and spicy garlic butter sauce, served with fries ... 24.
STEAK TARTARE OF PRIME FILET with haricots verts, Maui onions, artichoke and tomato
    salad, served with walnut wheat toast ... 24.
MARKET STREET MEATLOAF with spinach and mashed potatoes ... 16.
BOWL OF KICK ASS CHILI with cornbread and condiments ... 12.

SPECIALS

DINNER, SUNDAY, JULY 30

SOUP	CHILLED LEEK WITH YOGURT AND MINT ... 6.	
	RED GAZPACHO ... 6.	
OYSTER BAR	GRILLED MALPEQUE OYSTERS WITH SHALLOT, SHERRY	
	VINEGAR AND FRESH CORN SALAD ... 14.	
	TUNA SASHIMI WITH CALAMATA OLIVES, SUNDRIED	
	TOMATOES, LEMON, ARUGULA, AND	
	EXTRA VIRGIN OLIVE OIL ... 14.	
PASTA	FETTUCINE WITH CHICKEN, SWEET PEPPERS, TREE	
	MUSHROOMS, SUNDRIED TOMATOES,	
	GARLIC, OREGANO, SAUCE, NUT OIL ... 14.	
FISH	SAUTEED BAQUETTA SEA BASS WITH BASILLA CHILI,	
	BELL PEPPER, AND SWEET CORN	
	VINAIGRETTE ... 22.	
	GRILLED MAHI MAHI WITH LEMON CAPER BUTTER	
	SAUCE, SERVED ON A BED OF GARLIC	
	SPINACH ... 20.	
	GRILLED NORWEGIAN SALMON WITH DILL OIL AND	
	HONEY JOEY MUSTARD SAUCE ... 25.	
FOWL	GRILLED DUCK BREAST WITH LAURELS, BRANDY, AND	
	CREME FRAICHE, SERVED WITH WILD	
	RICE ... 24.	
MEAT	CURRIED LAMB WITH APPLE RAISIN CHUTNEY AND	
	SAUTEED SPINACH, SERVED WITH SAFFRON	
	RICE ... 30.	

Maple Drive
345 North Maple Drive, Beverly Hills

David (on phone to Annie): "It was a spur of the moment invitation? Anyone I know? That's fine—you guys go ahead and have a good lunch. I'll see you when I get home."
Agnes (to David): "She's not here. Said she's meeting someone for lunch at Maple Drive."
From "Eine Kleine Nacht Murder," Season 5, Episode 12

Maple Drive was also owned by the actor and director Tony Bill and the actor Dudley Moore. It was on the other side of town from Market Street, a few blocks from Rodeo Drive. It was located inside a high-tech office complex and opened in 1989.

Maple Drive was a trendy place to eat, the ultimate "Hollywood insider" restaurant. It was frequented by celebrities including Rob Reiner, Michelle Pfeiffer, Billy Crystal, and Ellen DeGeneres. Its most popular menu items included "kick ass chili"; Cajun-style meatloaf; grilled chicken with garlic, olive oil, and tomatillo salsa; and charred tuna with Japanese-style vinaigrette.[37]

345 North Maple Drive
Beverly Hills, CA 90210
213-274-9800

---

37 Ruth Reichl, "Where Success Is in the Details: Tony Bill's Maple Drive Offers Straightforward Fare in a Serene Beverly Hills Setting," *Los Angeles Times*, November 19, 1989.

Cocoanut Grove
Located inside the Ambassador Hotel
Moonlighting Wrap Party
(Closed 1989)

The Cocoanut Grove is famous in the *Moonlighting* Metaverse as the site of the *Moonlighting* wrap party in 1989. [38]

Cocoanut Grove was a nightclub inside the Ambassador Hotel on Wilshire Boulevard in Los Angeles that featured lavish, exotic décor. It opened in 1921 and closed its doors in 1989. It held about eight hundred people and was decorated with coconut trees, a bandstand, and a large dance floor. The club continued as a filming location until the hotel itself was demolished in 2006. The *Los Angeles Times* noted in its society column that "The Cocoanut Grove was probably the most beloved public room of all time."

The Cocoanut Grove was an important venue for performers like Bing Crosby, Ray Charles, Barbra Streisand, Dean Martin, Harry Belafonte, Judy Garland, and Diana Ross. The Oscars were hosted there several times, as were many celebrity-filled parties.

Many famous movies were filmed at the Ambassador Hotel, including

---

38 Curtis Armstrong, *Revenge of the Nerd*, Thomas Dunne Books, July 11, 2017.

The Graduate, LA Story, and Pretty Woman. Sadly, The Ambassador Hotel was also the site of Robert F Kennedy's assassination in 1968.

After a lot of public outcries to maintain the Ambassador Hotel as a historic site, it was demolished in 2005 and is now the site of the Robert F. Kennedy Community Schools Education Complex, with parts of the old hotel integrated into the new design—including the Cocoanut Grove, which has new life as an auditorium.[39]

---

39   PBS, "The Ambassador Hotel, Los Angeles," Things That Aren't Here Anymore, Episode 3, January 19, 2023, pbs.org.

– CHAPTER 7 –
THE STRAIGHT POOP

"The Straight Poop" is a season-three episode featuring the legendary celebrity columnist Rona Barrett that features many clips of Maddie and David throughout the series. This chapter is named after this episode and highlights some of the fun facts about food and drinks sprinkled throughout *Moonlighting* as well as the 1980s as a whole.

Perrier-Jouët

Every time a bottle of champagne is poured in *Moonlighting* – from the California Investigators' Association Annual Banquet and Ball in "North by North Dipesto" to dinner with Maddie's parents in "Every Daughter's Father Is a Virgin" to David and Maddie in the limo in "Symphony in Knocked Flat" to the toast to Agnes and Bert's engagement in "Lunar Eclipse"—it is a bottle of Perrier-Jouët.

Perrier-Jouët is a French champagne producer based in the Epernay region of Champagne. The company was founded in 1811 by Pierre-Nicolas Perrier and Rose-Adélaïde Jouët. It produces about three million bottles of its vintage and vintage champagne every year. It began shipping its champagne to the United States in 1837.[1]

The current floral bottle design was created in 1902 by Émile Gallé, one of the most famous glass and cabinet makers in the Art Nouveau style. The bottle is decorated with white and pale pink anemones with green stems and gold borders. It was designed to evoke the Belle Epoque era of the turn of the twentieth century.

In 2024, a bottle of Perrier-Jouët cost about $250, on par with other high-end champagnes such as Dom Pérignon. In terms of taste, Wine Spectator magazine says this champagne

---

1 "History of Champagne: Perrier-Jouët of France," *Middletown Press*, April 12, 2000.

is "elegant with a creamy, finely, meshed range of pastry cream, yellow apple, and pear, almond biscotti, elderflower, and preserved lemon flavors. Shows a rich underpinning of toast and smoke, with a frame of bright, delicate acidity. Long, plush finish."[2]

Stella Artois

Similarly, every time someone drinks a bottle of beer in *Moonlighting*, it is always a Stella Artois. Several bottles fall out of the BMW—along with David!—in "The Son Also Rises." David, Richie, and Walter are drinking it at Walter's bachelor party in "Maddie Hayes Got Married." David pulls one out of his fridge and drinks it in "And the Flesh Was Made Word."

Stella Artois is a pilsner beer that has been brewed in Leuven, Belgium, for over six hundred—since 1366! Stella Artois is owned by Interbrew International, a subsidiary of the world's largest brewer, Anheuser-Busch. Stella Artois is advertised as containing only four ingredients: hops, malted barley, maize, and water. In the 1980s, the Stella Artois advertising slogan was "Reassuringly Expensive," leading to its reputation as a higher-end beer. Stella Artois has been a primary sponsor of many film festivals, including Cannes and Sundance.[3]

---

2   "Perrier-Jouët: The History," Perrier Jouët, October 10, 2024, perrier-jouet.com.
3   "It's All in the Name," Stella Artois, October 10, 2024, stellaartois.com.

David Addison's Chocolate Milk and Alta Dena Dairy

David: "Close a case—gotta celebrate! We have chocolate milk!"
From "Atlas Belched," Season 2, Episode 9

David: "No use crying over spilt milk.[Then, to Maddie] Hit them with the cottage cheese. Go for the large curd!"
From "Maddie's Turn to Cry," Season 3, Episode 13

Agnes: "Mr. Addison! You're back! I stocked your refrigerator with chocolate milk!"
From "Father Knows Last," Season 4, Episode 7

David (to Maddie): "I have some things to do, so I'm going to go now. Unlike you, I will be back. There's cookies and milk in the fridge and movie money on the table. Whatever you do, don't leave. Don't marry someone else and don't divorce him."
From "And the Flesh Was Made Word," Season 4, Episode 14

There are countless references to milk, and especially chocolate milk, made throughout *Moonlighting*. In every instance in which a milk logo is seen in *Moonlighting*, it is Alta Dena Dairy milk, a local Southern California brand.

David Addison's love for chocolate milk is well established in *Moonlighting*. He and Agnes always keep his office refrigerator well stocked with it, and it is his favorite nonalcoholic drink. We see David enjoying chocolate milk in several episodes, including season two's "Atlas

Belched," season three's "Sam and Dave," and season four's "Cool Hand Dave, Part 1."

During the opening sequence of season one's "The Next Murder You Hear," we see Alta Dena Dairy milk being delivered—and bottles being broken while the viewer hears the sounds of gunshots broadcast in Paul McCain's radio show.

In season four's "Maddie's Turn to Cry," Maddie and David steal an Alta Dena Dairy milk delivery truck to chase down their client Elaine Johnson and her lover, Alan McClafferty, after learning his wife's death was not a suicide, but a murder. David drives while Maddie throws dairy products at their getaway car. The chase scene ends at a Los Angeles bowling alley.

There are countless other moments in *Moonlighting* when milk is mentioned. Richie—as Ed in Maddie's *Honeymooners* black-and-white dream sequence in season four's "A Trip to the Moon"—is drinking a glass of milk. In season four's "Tracks of My Tears," Maddie has nightmares about David turning into "nice, safe man" Pat Boone as a married man and father—and this version of "David" drinks plain white milk instead of chocolate milk. In season four's "Eek! A Spouse!" Maddie compares Walter to non dairy coffee creamer and David to real milk in her conversation with Agnes. And in season four's "Maddie Hayes Got Married," David talks to Maddie about the importance of a balanced diet for a pregnant woman, including grains, fruits, and milk. Even Blue Moon Shampoo itself is made from "milk and honey and a tablespoon of moonbeams".

Alta Dena Dairy opened in 1945 and provides dairy products to families across Southern California, including the greater Los Angeles area. It started out as a small, family dairy, but today it is a farmer-owned brand of Dairy Farmers of America (DFA), a cooperative of farmer-owners.[4]

---

4   "Our History—Alta Dena Dairy," October 10, 2024, altadenadairy.com.

Miss Dipesto's Grocery List

In "'Twas the Episode Before Christmas," Season 2, Episode 10, David and Maddie go to Agnes's apartment after Agnes and the baby go missing. There they meet the Three Kings and find that Agnes's cute rhymes also apply to her groceries:

>Get us some lettuce.
>Grab us some steak.
>Remember the cheese, please.
>And a box of Frosted Flakes.

Maddie's Cooking Class

In "Eine Kleine Nacht Murder," Season 5, Episode 12, Maddie—hoping to make better use of her state-of-the-art 1980s kitchen—takes an evening cooking class where she is learning how to make giblet gravy. She befriends a fellow classmate, who is a neurologist.

Cooking classes became extremely popular in the 1980s as people's desire to have more exotic dishes grew. Also, an explosion of new cookware, kitchen gadgets, and appliances was hitting the market, and home kitchens were becoming more state-of-the-art.

Maddie's friend: "Your first class?"
Maddie: "I have a great kitchen at home which I've never been in. It's time to learn to cook."
Maddie's friend: "Trying to catch a guy, huh?"
Maddie: "No actually, I'm not trying to catch a guy, but if I was trying to catch a guy, I wouldn't be looking for someone who wanted a scullery maid. You and I were not put on this earth to cook and clean."
And then later . . .
Maddie: "Boy, slicing, dicing, and stirring can really take it out of you."

Food Trends in the 1980s

The 1980s was a time of many trends and cultural shifts, and food and drinks were no exception. Dining out at higher-end and "celebrity chef" restaurants became very trendy in the 1980s as part of the Yuppie lifestyle and the economic boom of the decade. The 1980s also gave rise to the "foodie," a person passionate about dining out, cooking, and food trends.

American nouvelle cuisine, spa cuisine, and California cuisine became popular in the 1980s, as did Tex-Mex, Cajun, and Southwest-style foods. Cuisine from other cultures, especially Japanese, Italian, Russian, and Mexican, were also trendy in the 1980s. Pizzas with nontraditional toppings like BBQ or Thai chicken became popular along with the restaurants that served them, such as California Pizza Kitchen and Spago. We see Maddie and David embracing many of these trends throughout *Moonlighting*.[5]

Trendy food in restaurants in the 1980s included:

- Tiramisu
- Crème Brûlée
- Pesto and vodka pasta sauces
- Fajitas
- Blackened redfish
- Beurre Blanc Sauce
- Extra-virgin olive oil
- Honey mustard salad dressing
- Raspberry vinaigrette
- Mesquite-cooked meats and seafood
- Radicchio
- Warm goat cheese salads
- Pasta salad
- Sun Dried Tomatoes
- Sushi
- Frozen yogurt
- Edible flowers

---

5 "The 80s—From Nouvelle to Anything Goes," *Los Angeles Times*, December 24, 1989.

Convenience foods also became more popular in the 1980s. The microwave oven was a new addition to most American kitchens in the early to mid eighties, providing busy families with a quick way to heat meals. Prepared meals such as Lean Cuisine, Le Menu, and Budget Gourmet were introduced to supermarkets. Sales of frozen meals totaled $750 million in 1983 and continued to rise throughout the decade. Frozen meals catered to consumers' desire for convenience foods as well as diet and portion control. We see Maddie buying a Budget Gourmet entrée at a Safeway in season three's "Blonde on Blonde."

Brands and at-home foods introduced in the 1980s include:
- Microwave popcorn
- Lean Cuisine
- Snapple
- Diet Coke
- Reese's Pieces
- Hot Pockets
- McDonald's Chicken McNuggets
- Cinnamon Toast Crunch cereal
- Jell-O Pudding Pops
- Fruit Roll-Ups
- Jelly Belly
- Capri Sun
- Crystal Light
- Wine coolers

Epilogue

To all the *Moonlighting* fans out there: I hope you enjoy this cookbook! Make a drink and a meal from this book, sit back, and enjoy while watching your favorite episodes.

And remember . . .

"No tears, no fears
Remember there's always tomorrow
For parting is not goodbye
We'll be together again"

CAROLYN MERRITT GANDY

$-$ACKNOWLEDGMENTS$-$

Thank you to my husband, Darren, for his constant encouragement and support and for being a happy taste tester (and sometimes food critic) during the development of the recipes in this book.

Thank you to my father, Morris Emory Merritt, for giving me a lifelong love of television and film. Thanks for taking me to the movies every Saturday afternoon when I was young. And thanks for convincing me to watch the pilot episode of *Moonlighting* with you, igniting a lifelong love of this wonderful show.

Thank you to my children, Claire and Clark, for their encouragement and ideas and for turning out to be the most wonderful, interesting, creative people, who love television and films as much as their father and I do. And special thanks to Claire for creating the book cover art.

Thank you to my lifelong friends Lori and Nancy for always supporting me in my sometimes quirky interests and endeavors—and for listening to me talk about *Moonlighting* for the past forty years!

Thank you to Lori and David for being such great friends who are always happy to discuss food, recipes, restaurants, movies, and television. And thanks to Lori for her sugar cookie recipe, which is featured in this book.

Thank you to all of my Blue *Moonlighting* friends who have been so supportive of this project—especially to Danielle for encouraging me to write this book; to Norene, Laurel, and Josh for being dear Moonie friends; and to Laurie for helping me get in touch with my publishers.

Thank you to my wonderful editors at Tucker DS Press, David and Scott, for editing and publishing this book.

Thanks to Shawna, Grace, and Scott for their extensive *Moonlighting* knowledge and for being trailblazers with their own *Moonlighting* books (and podcast), which have been invaluable to me in my own research for this book—and such a joy for this *Moonlighting* fan to read (and listen to).

Thank you to the entire *Moonlighting* team—cast, crew, writers, producers, and directors—for this magical show that has brought such joy to so many of us. A special thanks to Glenn Gordon Caron for being the creator and mastermind behind *Moonlighting*. I can't begin to express the admiration and respect that I have for you. And thank you to Cybill Shepherd, Bruce Willis, Allyce Beasley, and Curtis Armstrong for bringing the characters of Maddie, David, Agnes, and Bert to life and giving them such brilliance and depth.

This book is dedicated to all the *Moonlighting* fans out there. I hope you enjoy reading this book and trying out the recipes as much as I did creating them.

–ABOUT THE AUTHOR–

Carolyn Merritt Gandy has been an avid fan of *Moonlighting* since it first began airing in 1985. She has a lifelong love of television and film and worked for decades in television and media, focusing on rights, licensing, and technology. She was, as part of a team at Turner Broadcasting, a recipient of a 2015 Technical Emmy Award for Pioneering Development of Data Driven Traffic Systems in Multichannel Environments.

Carolyn is a graduate of the University of Georgia and a lifelong resident of the metro Atlanta area. She and her husband, Darren, have two grown children, Claire and Clark, and a cute but opinionated corgi, Elphaba.

In her spare time, Carolyn enjoys watching television and movies, hiking, traveling, reading, and cooking. She is a self-professed foodie and enjoys creating new recipes and going out to restaurants.

MORE "MOONLIGHTING" BOOKS

Order these two other *Moonlighting* books available now at TuckerDSPress.com

ALSO AVAILABLE FROM FMP/TUCKER DS

ORDER AT TUCKERDSPRESS.COM

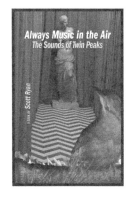

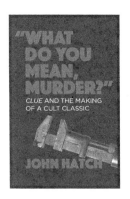

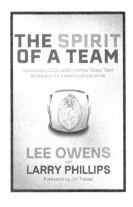